THE SHAME
OF LOSING

THE SHAME OF LOSING

∽०∾

A MEMOIR

Sarah Cannon

 Red Hen Press | *Pasadena, CA*

Book layout by Amber Lucido

ISBN: 978-1-59709-624-9

Library of Congress Control Number: 2018031084

The National Endowment for the Arts, the Los Angeles County Arts
Commission, the Ahmanson Foundation, the Dwight Stuart Youth
Fund, the Max Factor Family Foundation, the Pasadena Tournament
of Roses Foundation, the Pasadena Arts & Culture Commission and
the City of Pasadena Cultural Affairs Division, the City of Los Angeles
Department of Cultural Affairs, the Audrey & Sydney Irmas Charitable
Foundation, the Kinder Morgan Foundation, the Meta & George Rosen-
berg Foundation, the Allergan Foundation, the Riordan Foundation,
and the Amazon Literary Partnership partially support Red Hen Press.

First Edition
Published by Red Hen Press
www.redhen.org

ACKNOWLEDGMENTS

I would like to dedicate this book to my late Nana whose love for books and family will always be with me. The second dedication is for my Mom & Dad, who have been there for all of it. I love you. Thank you to everyone at Red Hen Press, especially Monica Fernandez, Keaton Maddox, Rebeccah Sanhueza, and Kate Gale. To my mentors in the Creative Writing program at Goddard College—Aimee Liu, Darrah Cloud, and Ryan Boudinot—thank you. Heartfelt appreciation for Jessamyn Smyth for the time at Quest Writer's Conference in Squamish, B.C., and for Rebecca Brown, my mentor there. The constant encouragement provided by writers and readers Samantha Kolber Pyatak, Ginna Richardson Luck, Julie Shayne, Heather Ohly, and Francine Walsh has made my finishing this book possible. And for proof that friendship can lift you up, thank you to my closest ones—you know who you are. For their profound support, I wish to thank Ned and Maura Cannon. Last and most importantly, I want to express my deep-felt respect for Miles, whose strength in survival we might all look toward when life throws us sideways, my least favorite word. Memory is fickle and contestable. This version is only mine.

Thank you to the editors who published essays of which parts or themes of which appear in this book: Dan Jones at the *New York Times*; Sarah Hepola at Salon.com; Abby Murray at *Collateral Journal*.

Credits: Dr. Jill Bolte Taylor, Lee Woodruff & Bob Woodruff, Erich Maria Remarque, Frank Ocean, Norah Jones, UW Harborview Medical Center, Kevin Pierce & Crash Reel, Brain Injury Alliance of Washington, Mark O'Brien & *The Sun Magazine*, Thich Nhat Hanh, and Yue Minjun.

For Eliza and Will and childhood survivors everywhere.

PART I

On October 30, 2007, I was volunteering at a local arts center in our suburb, preparing for an auction. Halloween was the next day and I was thinking about our five-year-old daughter Lizzie's oversized, pink cowgirl costume. Isaac, just two and a half, was going as Superman. My husband Matt, a crew lead for an arboriculture company, would meet us after work at my parents' house in Magnolia, a neighborhood in Seattle. He and his team were planning to remove a bigleaf maple in Issaquah. I came back to my desk and assumed the three missed calls meant Matt was trying to reach me regarding domestic logistics. Should he pick up a flank steak? Did we need milk? I didn't bother listening to the messages and called him right back. But Matt's co-worker, young Teddy, answered.

"Oh God," he was saying, over and over.

I could hear moaning in the background and a siren.

"Stay still, Matt," Teddy was saying. My mouth, so dry, formed words that sounded oddly natural.

"What happened?"

"Jesus," Teddy said. "His cheekbones are *sideways*."

I created an image of Matt's brain drowning in blood, his face smashed to pieces. Teddy was talking to the EMTs who said for me to meet them at the hospital. "Harborview," Teddy told me, the hospital downtown. Don't let him die, I begged silently. I ran to my car, my throat sensationally dry, like there was a small kitchen cloth towel shoved down deep inside. I wanted to gag. Val, my boss, saw me grab my coat and purse in a panic and followed after me as I ran.

"Is it the kids?" she shouted. I shook my head no: it was my husband. There had been an accident. It was serious.

Val helped me fish my keys from my purse. The landscape was like a blurry mirage and she shook my arms and said, "Do you know how to get to Harborview?" I nodded yes and asked, screamed, for everyone to please pray. I sounded foreign to myself, panicked and lost. Driving to the emergency room, my lips went from cold, to cold and itchy, to cold and itchy and rubbery. My hands trembled but there was this keenness in my mind, as if something outside my body was dialing in a necessary focus, and I heard these words on replay, like a roll of tape, a succession of thoughts: *OK, he's badly hurt. But Teddy said he was moving. If he's hurt, please don't let it be so bad he can't recover.*

I pulled into the hospital's roundabout entrance and let my SUV idle. I hopped out and dangled the car keys at two calm uniformed men. One helped me with my car and the other escorted me to the social worker area. The intake lady sat me in one of the baby blue plastic scooped seats. The whole place smelled like urine. Street people made up the bulk of people waiting. The intake lady clicked her acrylic nails over her keyboard and used a yellow walkie-talkie. I heard fuzzy static in my inner ear.

This was Harborview, where a friend had her stomach pumped in seventh grade; where my friend's brother got treated after an assault with a baseball bat at a house party; where a family friend's child was flown from Whistler after he snapped his vertebrae skiing. It is a Level I trauma center, the highest level of care for all serious injuries and burns, serving patients from Washington, Montana, Alaska, and Idaho. It is the place, someone would tell me later, where half the arrivals end up in the county morgue.

I had taken great care with my outfit that morning. I wore a black, floor-length wrap skirt, knee-length wool socks, engineer boots, and a thin cashmere hoodie. I sat there freezing. The social worker had cold hands with large veins. She led me into a private waiting area and gave me a warm blanket to stop my uncontrollable shivering. I would need to wait here for a few more minutes; he'd only just arrived, and that was all the information she had. I couldn't talk, so I nodded. I signed some papers and nodded when she asked if I had family to contact. Does Matt have parents? I said yes, his mother lives in Salem. She wanted me to call her and I shook my head: no.

"The thing is," she said, "if he passes on she will want to know when it happened, and trust me, you don't want to have to tell her you waited on news of the accident."

I was in the epicenter of horror and I understood. I would do it, I assured her. Then she left me. Sitting there alone I felt abandoned by the world. What God would do this? What kind of life would we be living? I doubled over, making myself as small as I could, hugging my own body like I used to as a small child. She returned and walked me through swinging doors and long bright corridors to see him. Matt was the only patient behind the green vinyl curtain. His sweatshirt was cut open and electrodes were stickered to his perfect chest. Nurses tended to him and I hardly wept because he looked so beautiful. His work-wear jeans were soiled with chainsaw gas, and wood chips laced the inside ankle cuffs. The nurses stared at me as I stared at him.

"He's comfortable," they offered. "He can't feel any pain."

A ring of blood lined his ears and fresh drips leaked from his eyes. They talked about brain bleed. They talked about subdural hematoma. They talked about blunt force trauma. I didn't know what any of it meant. They said he'd be there for a while and there would be surgeries. But they were positive. They said, "He's young and strong." I couldn't see what the professionals saw: a skull crumpled, a blown-out eye, busted eye sockets, and a collapsed nose.

Important surgeons came and flooded me with details. One said Matt would be blind and I blinked, waiting for better details. They wore suits under white coats and nice leather shoes. To measure the intracranial pressure, they'd need to drill into his skull and attach a monitor. None of this was a joke; it was not a bad dream. I heard the blade rev as the social worker led me out of triage. It was better if I was not there, they said. Was it my imagination, or did I truly inhale dry smoke, the smell of serrated metal slicing into skull bones? I felt my lungs struggling to pump air, to breathe normally. My stomach was clenched, empty, carved out.

Back in the family room, a young female chaplain was waiting for me, along with my dad. My mom came. She massaged my shoulders and whispered soothing words in my ear. Matt's mom Joanna had a five-hour-long drive north. The details were lucid—I was one with the dim lamp with the yellowish glow; I was one with the wadded-up tissues in the wire basket; I was one with the stains on the sink basin in the bathroom. Other families who had had similar phone calls lingered in the hallways, but we didn't

make eye contact, we didn't talk. The matriarchs demanded cold packs and water and medical notes and phone calls.
My brother and his wife would come later, but not in that
room. That little room was for me. It was the home of the
beginning of something new I didn't want. I turned my cell
phone off. I just wanted to go home to the children.

This little book will not always be so sad. For example, my
childhood.

When I was a girl my mom would send me with my dad
to his work shipyard. My dad's office was a quick drive from
the home we had by the Ballard Locks, a water canal that
provides navigable connection for ships traveling between
salty Puget Sound and freshwater Lake Washington. It was
always a special treat to ride alongside Dad in the '46 Chevy
pickup, the truck that would become a father-son weekend
restoration project, the truck that would eventually be my
wheels for high school.

Dad's work trailer on West Commodore Way smelled
like blueprint ink and pencil shavings. Inside, I would drift
from the drafting table in his private office to the open area
of his colleagues—guys like Franz, the German who kept
chocolate wafer cookies under his desk, or Guillermo, the
Chilean with thick eyebrows, or Stevie, the kooky fellow
who whistled songs through his teeth. There were the junior
drafters who ignored me except to say hi at the water cooler.
There was always a nice secretary up front who would give
me a coloring book or a semi-melted candy bar from her desk
drawer. At home during dinner, dad would balk at downtown office jobs where designers never saw their ships being
built. He needed to walk through the bowels of the hull.

"You have to actually *talk* to the welders," he would say.

At christenings for a gleaming new tug, the buyer and his wife would smash champagne over the bow and cut the red ribbon while my brother and I huddled under an umbrella in a downpour. I always wanted to shout, "My dad made that boat!" at the crowd. It always felt like *our* boat, built against the hours he was gone.

On weekends, Dad would drag my brother and me to Ernst Hardware to shop for spark plugs, turpentine, or GOOP hand cleaner. If it wasn't Ernst, we might travel downtown to West Marine, where he and the manager would discuss best and worst bilge pumps, chart plotters, shackles, snaps and fittings. It was boring. I would hold my pee and hover around the gumball machine, collecting leftover Chiclets from inside the little trap of the metal door.

Inside Dad's checked dress shirt pocket in those early years was always a calculator and a set of mechanical pencils. At home on the top deck was a telescope for stargazing and a set of binoculars. We had a hardbound set of Encyclopedia Britannica, and there was a table saw in the garage. I was too small to remember every detail, but I remember loving that first house. It was the loveliest shade of blue. We had a jungle gym in the backyard and all the elderly single women in the neighborhood gave us cookies and wrapped chocolates from special glass jars.

"Your father is such a nerd," my mother would say at dinner. She said it with a fond note in her voice. They loved each other a lot.

I was never shy about not wanting to go to the shipyard on Saturdays. I'd lock myself in the bathroom until he was forced to leave without me. I wasn't shy with much around my family. A story goes around that once, in church, a young pastor asked the congregation if we thought his sermon was nice. I was sitting under the pew and took a stab at the truth. It is said (I don't remember) that I sat up and screamed, "NO!" No, it wasn't nice, and everyone had to hear about it. For me, roads with yellow street signs that read DEAD END were where beleaguered street people went to die. I didn't want to be beleaguered. I didn't want to die. We lived down one of those roads, and I was suspicious of the end of it, so I avoided it until I was about ten. I nicknamed our family cross-country skiing adventures *uphill skiing* because our parents made us climb with our skis on our backs toward the trails at Snoqualmie Pass. We wanted to go downhill skiing like the cool kids with money, but if you asked my parents why they didn't want to buy us lift tickets, they'd ask you why you were asking. It was so simple to them: why would someone buy lift tickets when hiking was free? Outhouses were *robbers' bathrooms* fit only for criminals who stole things from small children. I used to fall asleep under the spell of the family dentist's hypnotic voice. In high school, I squeezed my thighs into super thick tannish hosiery and a sports skirt for the school Flags team. In college, I shaved my long hair and bleached the leftover fuzz platinum; I resembled a scarecrow and wore a T-shirt that read HERE COMES TROUBLE.

I'm not sure of this notion of people changing over the course of their lives. Some days I think people change, and other times I think our core is our core. On days when I feel like that punky girl at church, I wonder how Matt put up with me at all. It says a lot about Matt that these were the things about me that he thought were funny. It says a lot about what privilege I was afforded. Matt teased me all the time and I liked that. It felt familiar, like a good older brother, or a safe dad.

Before we continue, I need to tell you the story of Keith, Matt's father. It was late summer in 1974 and a fire was burning in Oregon's Willamette National Forest. Keith was piloting an AStar 510 helicopter positioned to take off from a tight landing zone, preparing to pick up two smoke-jumpers. Did the engine fail? Had he taken off downwind? Who knows? All we know is that the machine crashed into a tree and that Keith was twenty-five when he was killed. We know that tree branches cracked through the front windows and he was found with one pierced through his heart. We know that Keith had learned to fly in the service, trading Vietnam orders with a guy who wanted war pay in exchange for a station in Korea. We know he was a loving husband and a good son and brother.

This too seems like a joke, or a dream. Imagine Matt's mother, just twenty-four. It wasn't a phone call; it was a knock at the door. It was a sheriff delivering nightmare news. Matt was born a few months later in a Salem hospital to a terrorized mother. A few hundred miles north, I was a newborn in a Seattle hospital—a younger sister, the perfect addition to a nuclear unit.

Twenty-five years later, Joanna couldn't talk about Keith's death without tearing up. This was hard for me to understand, and yet I tried to be cool—a lot had happened. Possibly a result of trauma, Matt and his mom seemed like siblings, far closer than my notion of a *regular* relationship between parent and child. They talked on the phone every day. I was jealous. She would cry to him over her problems and I'd sit and listen and roll my eyes. When we became serious as a couple, Matt warned me how his mom could be difficult.

"She does this dumb blonde thing, but really, she's whip-smart," he told me.

Matt was a quiet guy, but during long car rides, he'd consider the impact of his father's tragic death. He would say stuff like, "Maybe her trauma altered my biochemistry. Like maybe the fight-or-flight hormones she experienced electrified me with adrenaline."

As his wife, I would come to agree with his theory, especially years later, when it became clear he not only had a thrill-seeking gene, but an accident-prone one as well. I always wanted to write about his fascinating family history—not the trauma, but the connection both sides of his family have with woods and machines and Oregon. I had never known anyone with roots that deep in one area.

After his accident, instead of contemplating what it meant to be a forester in Oregon, I would lie in bed and vow to stop what seemed like a generational trauma. Sleepless and obsessed, I would assert to the universe that occupational injuries would end with our children.

Matt commended Joanna for having endured the unendurable. At the same time, because he is as full and flawed a human as all of us, he complained a lot about her being clingy. (She was.) He resented it when she said things like, "It's just you and me against the world, son." He didn't want to be his mom's BFF. This was a relief to me.

Joanna remarried and had another son, but Matt never called anyone Dad. His step-dad was OK. He had a nice family. They all nicknamed Matt "Nick Danger" because he liked to ski real fast downhill. Indeed, he was the proud holder of a special award from his high school ski team that said, "What's a turn?" He was that guy. And I loved him.

It's still so clear to me, the scene when Matt called his mother to break the news of our engagement. We were in the kitchen of our rented house in the hilly suburbs of Portland when she asked to please speak with me. I wanted to speak to her. I thought she wanted to congratulate us, and I wanted to gush and say thanks. But Matt tried to protect me, saying I was busy in the kitchen. Stupidly, and because I was young, I demanded he hand me the phone.

"Listen," she said. "I know you two are in love, but I'm not ready to lose him yet."

I didn't know what to say.

"You've heard the saying. When you have sons and they get married they leave you forever."

I still didn't know what to say. I probably just told her, "OK," but I'm really not sure.

It was odd because my parents had acted completely the opposite, like they were so ready to let me go. I was the youngest, and a girl, and of appropriate childbearing age. My parents had always been responsible with their jobs and money and plans. They had each other to talk to; they were a team in a similar way Matt and Joanna were. Joanna had had her own mother-in-law issues with Keith and told me all about it.

"When I got married," she said, "Rose told me blood was thicker than water. She wasn't ready to lose her son, either."

I guessed some mothers were just like that. Mine called Joanna *codependent*, and later, other things.

I supposed without a dad you could still learn about metal and heat. I thought it was super cute when Matt became excited talking about helicopters. He'd point to the sky and call them out by name.

"That's the Bell 205," he'd say. "I flew that over the cherry orchards in Eastern Washington."

Joanna passed down Keith's man things. Keith's army-issued standard flight suit either hung in a closet or lived in a clear tub in the attic. Inside the collar was a worn label that said, "Coveralls, Flyers, Men, Summer, Fire Resistant, 27/P, Sage Green." Keith was a 44 Long, just like Matt. If you got close enough you could see the last name, Kishpaugh, stitched in a black bold on the right side of the chest pocket. Keith's flight bomber jacket was the kind that goes in and out of fashion: silky green on the outside with a bright orange interior. On the left breast was a plastic slip for the wearer's pilot's license, and on the right, a patch that said, "Luke," presumably Keith's flight nickname, and the acronym, IFR, which I presume stands for Instrument Flight Rules. There was also a patch that said, "HI FP 118 Assault Helicopter Company," and a picture of a guy's fist with lightning bolts coming out of the knuckles, behind it a white mountain with crooked peaks. Matt would say, "I know it's a sad story, but you don't have to feel sorry for me. I never knew him, so I don't really know what I'm missing."

He must have been used to telling the story of his father's tragic death. I would think about sentimental stuff and feel bad, and also fascinated, imagining how it must feel to be singled out for not having a dad when Father's Day came around in elementary school and everyone decorated a silly tie or made a special card. But that was me—I loved my dad and couldn't imagine life without him. My reaction was to not believe Matt when he acted all casual about it. I even accused him of dismissing the loss.

"Maybe I just don't want to hear myself complain," he would say. So fucking stoic.

It might be my imagination, because I don't have the actual photograph to show for this memory, but I remember a color photograph of Joanna sitting on the couch in her parents' living room in Eugene. Baby Matt is on her lap. She is slouched in the corner of the nubby mustard-colored sofa. On her side of the sofa is a stained hand-knitted cloth arm protector. Matt is frozen in an arching flail. Her dark blonde hair is greasy and limp. She wears a light pink floor-length robe that zips and has quilt batting. There is a tidy stack of wood in front of the iron stove by young Joanna's feet. She is holding a bottle and she is barefoot and there are hollowed circles beneath her eyes. Her direct unsmiling gaze reminds me of a wounded animal.

I used to think of that photograph when I got mad about Matt's accident, and the stress it caused in our marriage. I'd think to myself, *man, losing your beloved to a tragic accident with a baby on the way?* Matt had outlived his father, who had gone down in that firefighting blaze a hero. My husband may have been jobless, tired and confused, but at least he was alive. It's shameful, but everyone does it. We make comparisons to worse tragedies all the time. It's something

I try to be careful of now, knowing how it doesn't change reality, or work in any case, to make you feel less alone.

Matt and I met when we were nineteen. It was on a city bus ride in Lane, where hordes of hippies were coming back into town after a weekend at the Country Fair.

I was in college and he wasn't. I knew Matt's friend from the dorms, and he made introductions. Matt heaved his huge overnight pack up and gave me his seat. They'd been camping for days and Matt's neck reminded me of a smoke-stack. I saw a lanky guy with forearms that bulged like Pop-eye's. His dark blue eyes were clear and he stared at me as though he really knew me, holding an intense gaze longer than boys that age do.

That night, I got a call from his friend on the bus. Did us girls want to go to a party at their house? Yes, yes we did. We arrived on our cruiser bikes, because that's what we did in 1993. The walls of one room were covered in shag carpet and the ceiling was plastered with beer bottle caps. In the base-ment, snowboards were wallpaper. The only other girl at the party was wrestling with two boys in the living room. The gangster rap was blasting and there were some empty Pizza Hut boxes stacked tall in the kitchen.

I had just left the height of the grunge rock era in Se-attle, so I was pretty used to dingy hovels; in fact, I sought them out. I sort of liked grime. My college girlfriend from L.A., however, tugged on my arm once we browsed the joint, hissing in my ear *we should split*. But Matt found me. He cupped my hand softly before my friend convinced me *we should really go*. He and I talked on the porch and shared a cigarette before my roommate pushed me in the direction of our bikes. It was a quick goodbye. I regretted not having hugged him, especially when I heard he had left to fight forest fires on the east side of the mountains. I would scold him later, saying he should have at least asked for my phone number. I would have written him a letter, had he asked. I loved letters. He was a mystery to me, and I loved mysteries. I was nineteen.

A year later we began to date, or that's what I called it. He more or less still had a girlfriend. Having selected a college a state away from my parents was exciting, but I was lonely, so it was comforting that Matt seemed to know all the cool people. Once, he took me to his friend's parents' farm outside of town. It was a group of us and the plan was to spend the day picking flowers and fruit, make dinner, sleep outside. I thought this family lived a fascinating lifestyle, growing their own food and flowers and inviting guests to sleep in a massive Tepee alongside the river. My dress was a used, filmy, floor-length blue flowery tank-top gown I had found on 11th Street at St. Vincent de Paul. A breeze moved the bare threads of the dress over my skin and I saw him watching, his bandanna, his ruddy neck and broad smile and Nordic dimples. It was sincere when he dotted my hair with zinnias and called me Pocahontas. After the naked river plunge and before dinner, I fingered my necklace and shucked corn for the feast.

Is it corny, this young love? Yes, it is, and we do it, we imagine rearing chubby tan children who remind us of the one we love, or lust. Could we live on a farm outside of town like this? Yes, we could! We could sell flowers at the Saturday Market and host parties with drums and I could learn to sew hemp skirts.

Later, on the nubby green couch at my rental house back by the university, we kissed, and finally did the things I will not be telling you about here.

He didn't call. I let a month pass, and then decided to ride my bike in the rain to see him. I had not been invited. He was house-sitting for his ex-girlfriend while she was with her dad's tree-planting crew. I knew of the girl. She had see-through eyes and never smiled. I knew I was the perfect antidote to his heartache, but from his expression at the door when he let me in, either he didn't agree, or with my slicked hair and grease-stained pants he thought little more of me than a wet rat in the rain. He brought me an old towel, then stuffed wood into the fire. When he left to chop wood out back, I peeked at his journal tucked in the bedside table drawer.

There they were, words penciled in small careful capitalized letters: "I DON'T KNOW WHAT DO," he had written. "I'M IN LOVE WITH TWO WOMEN WHO ARE SMART AND BEAUTIFUL AND WHO BOTH WANT ME."

Of course, this made me want him more. I flipped the framed photo of the ex over and strutted around the living room in one of his white T-shirts. We made love and afterward he got up and made nachos. It was nice to have something other than tofu, and to play house like that. I never wanted to leave.

He said, "Don't you have somewhere you need to be?"

I shoved his T-shirt inside my bag and biked home, swaying sadly to Sarah McLachlan on my Walkman. I was heartbroken, but there was no solid reason to stay mad. He'd been earnest, saying he still loved her.

A few weeks later he wrote me an *I'm sorry* note, left on my front stoop inside a small wooden box, along with a handful of glass beads he'd spun himself. I heard a month later he left town again, this time for Montana—no ex by his side, just lone-ranger style. I crushed on how he was earning real-life experiences, paying his way as a grown-up, while I lived in financial protection, working a few hours a week at an old-fashioned hamburger joint.

Five years later, email was a thing and I initiated communication, saying, "Hey, so-and-so told me you're a helicopter pilot now . . . very cool! Any chance you want a visitor?" I'm pressing fast-forward on many years, you understand, but this is the only way to say it. We were young lovers, and then we weren't. We reconnected with the thrill of knowing we had always been fond of the other despite the girlfriends or boyfriends or whatever. It was the healthiest kind of rekindling of romance I can imagine.

Matt was naturally mechanical. Like my dad, he followed his father's legacy, except instead of an engineering degree, Matt earned his helicopter's license. He had a credit card with a zero balance and cash savings enough to buy me a simple diamond ring. After my risky international travels and list of noncommittal boyfriends, I'll bet his stable intent was refreshing to my parents, who I felt worried too much over my lack of ambition.

"By the time I am thirty-five," Matt told me early on in our courtship, "I will net eighty grand a year."

It slipped from his lips unfeigned; it wasn't a brag. Outside of Matt, my parents had rarely made any note of my love interests except to rebuff them. I also had this feeling that they didn't trust me to make it on my own. My mom would glorify young parenting. She said things that confused me, like, "You have so much energy when you're young, and once you find someone with similar goals, you have your whole lives together." She wanted me to fall in love, of course, and it was never about a man with money. But when Matt and I met and fell in love and he talked to my parents about the *future* future—buying property, investing in stocks—my mother likely looked at his clear blue eyes and thought, grandbabies, yes, and Sarah, secured.

A month or so into wedding planning my dad choked looking at my mom's credit card balance. Were we sure we wanted this? He made us an offer: a party or money for a small down payment. Now that I'm a parent, and much older, I can understand the practicality of this option. I can also understand just how privileged I was to have choices like these. Why do young adults want to blow money on a party, when it's just a day? It's generous to offer your child a small down payment for a home, which is long-term, rather than fund a big party, which you eat. But back then it hurt to think we couldn't have a party, a real celebration.

I squeaked out something like, "Sure, yeah, we can just do something small, like just go to the beach with our families," then put the phone down and went to my room and wept.

The thing is, I wanted my cousins and aunts there. My dad's sisters were married. My mom's brothers were married. My grandparents were married. They all lived in Michigan and my whole life we went out there for summers where we played in warm lakes and made up dance routines and had barbeques on the deck. In Seattle, it was just the four of us—my mom, dad, older brother and I. We were a tight nucleus and had enviable camping and boating adventures, but without extended family, I felt I was missing out. I wanted everyone to travel to see this impressive man I was choosing to spend my life with. I hadn't known I felt that way until I was faced with the alternative. I think my mom understood this. My dad called me back and apologized, saying they'd do their best.

We got married in early fall, when we were both a few months shy of twenty-six. It's so young, isn't it? My maternal grandmother had kept one of her mother's cocktail dresses from when she and her husband used to party in New York City. Lauretta was her name, and apparently, she was quite a woman, cutting her hair short and smoking in public. She graduated from Wellesley College in Massachusetts in 1914. Growing up, my mother called her Mère, in acknowledgment of our small bit of French heritage. The lace dress had three-quarter-length sleeves that belled out with delicate cloth buttons exposing a bare back. It hung in my mom's closet and its '20s aesthetic inspired my whole vision for our wedding. We found a seamstress to transform it into more of a gown, with a light pink silk tank sheath for underneath. My mom passed down an heirloom pearl bracelet with a diamond on the clasp.

The day before the wedding, my cousin gave me a Tiffany & Co. sterling silver necklace with a heart-shaped pendant. Matt and his buddies chartered a boat and caught the salmon we ate at the rehearsal dinner held at Matt's aunt's house.

Joanna embarrassed Matt when she organized a bizarre theatre performance with her actor friend who dressed up in a dog costume and made everyone howl at the moon and "kiss" their "paws," a word play on Matt's last name—soon mine. Matt complained afterward, "Why couldn't she just reserve the back room at some restaurant like I asked?" I was reluctant to comment on the strange things his mother did those days. It was important to be cordial; this woman was going to be family.

I woke at my parents' place the next morning and was relieved when the curtains opened to a cloudless sky. The ceremony was at a quiet city park atop a bluff overlooking Puget Sound. Friends read poetry and my uncle sang and played his guitar. Matt and I stayed strong when we read our crafted vows, but right after the ceremony, before people surrounded us in congratulations, we held a moment of quiet weeping. We looked into each other's eyes. We'd meant everything we'd said to each other and sharing it with our community made it real. My brain buzzed from all that attention and my cheeks hurt from smiling, but having this moment, a sense of peaceful stillness filled my heart. Life could begin now—this was it.

After the ceremony, our four best friends met at the shipyard where my dad moored his 1974 diesel cruiser. The women sipped champagne and the men swilled from flasks as my dad motored us into Lake Union, inching along at eight knots per hour until we were greeted at the dock with fanfare. We slow-danced to our first song, and afterward I twirled around with my dad while Matt entertained the matriarchs. Matt had grown up next door to the rabbi's family and knew more about Judaism than Christianity.

His friends lifted us up on chairs over their shoulders and we sang and danced the Hava Nagila. We were sweaty when we cut the three-tiered cake sprinkled with the red and pink rose petals from my bouquet. Matt removed my silky blue lace bridal garter and slung it into the crowd and I laughed to see my girlfriends fighting over my tossed bouquet on the floor. Everyone I loved was there. I was so happy I forgot to eat, so later we got burgers at Dick's on 45th.

The next day, we used bungee cords to secure our gifts in the bed of Matt's pickup with a blue tarp. We would drop off our stuff at our apartment in Portland then head to the coast for a long weekend. I sniffed the salty air of my girlhood home. Listening to the gulls squawking, I was overcome with emotion and began to bawl. I confused myself. This was supposed to be the happiest time of my life, right? We had so much going for us—I was sure there would be babies and a house and my mom would help and my dad would take us sailing. So why did I feel like I was losing something at the same time I was gaining so much? Maybe my aunt had been right. "Your dad is sad tonight," she told me as we drove to my girlfriend's house to kick off the bachelorette party the Friday before the wedding. I thought for a second she was referring to my skimpy outfit for the club. But looking at her I could tell that wasn't it.

"He is losing you," she had said. "Everything changes when you get married."

The low grasses at the beach were deep violet and the rolling dunes were honey in the sinking sun. One night as Matt and I walked along the empty beach shore the weather closed in on us. The sand bits were like enemy granules the way they smashed into our flushed cheeks. Matt tried to protect me with his sweatshirt and we made a game of it, army-crawling toward safety beneath the stir of the small cyclone. The next day was sunny again. The air smelled like blackberries and I climbed a tree. He peered up my skirt and made corny jokes. We popped champagne, we fed each other grapes. We took half-nude photos and held hands along the boardwalk. Older couples stopped us and took our picture.

They said, "You must be on your honeymoon."

◆ ◆ ◆

11/03/2007
4:00 PM

Hannah gave me this special notebook and a nice pen so I'm gonna start documenting stuff for myself. There's another one in Matt's room that anyone can write in—it's more like a guestbook. He gets a lot of visitors and it will be nice for people to add little notes, so that in a few months when he is better he can read it all and be inspired. I'll start by saying something about what's happening outside the hospital. One, it's my birthday. To celebrate my thirty-third birthday my friends went totally over the top and bought a dozen of these delicate craft cupcakes I can't eat because obviously, I have no appetite. I brought them to the nurses' station because I really want the nurses to love me so they will love Matt so they can do their jobs. Before all of this we weren't prayer people, but now when I'm with the kids in the car we always pray, especially when we see an ambulance. We pray for the nurses and doctors to get good nights of sleep so they can do their jobs. At night, I just want to melt into their little bodies, or meditate on the wall in the living room at my mom's. Isaac colored a spot on the wall with a red crayon. The mark is like a bullseye or a touchstone or something, a mark that reminds me to remind me to remind me to remind me. It helps me focus is what I'm trying to say. Please, I say to it, please just let the nurses get sleep tonight so they can do their jobs. Shoot, I know I said I had two things to report—wait, did I?—but now I can't remember the second. I don't care that it's my birthday. But I am a little worried I might be going nuts. One of Matt's mom's friends told me I was going to need the patience of an angel and it really FREAKED me out. She gave me a sparkly pink shawl and told me to drape it over my shoulders. She said it was God's protection. It kinda makes me feel like a gypsy, especially since she doused it with patchouli oil. But I wear it every day. And I smell it and think about tree sap and gasoline. I am OK with people praying for us. The energy is BIG and I can feel myself with every breath a little lighter, like I'm lifted, floating.

11/05/2007
2:00 AM

The monitors are gone. He's moving from the SICU. It's daylight savings. We get an extra hour. I have these little cards someone gave me; they're 1" x 1" squares you flip open for an uplifting quote. They're silky, not matte, so they feel good on my fingers. I fondle them at night. The children have been scribbling on them. They say BELIEVE on the front. I don't recognize most of the authors' names, but I like this one a lot, by Graham Greene, who I liked reading in college: "There is always one unexpected little moment when a door opens to let the future in." I doubt he meant something like what's happening in here, or maybe he did. Either way, all of it, no matter who you are, is unexpected and the future will happen no matter what. I wrote on the back of the little card, "You are fighting the doctors; you pulled out your NG tubes." You're so strong, Matt. I love you.

11/07/2007
9:00 AM

Last night I stayed up late eating a box of Wheat Thins with cream cheese for dinner. I emptied a bottle of wine while my dad figured out Matt's pay stubs to submit for a workers' compensation claim. Supposedly, the Division of Workers' Compensation will pay us about $4,000 a month, which is 65 percent of Matt's average earnings, which will be OK for a while. It was embarrassing to share pay stubs with my dad, but he was impressed at Matt's earnings, which made me feel proud. I'm worried this means I will have to go back to work. How will I do that and take care of Matt and kids at the same time? My mom keeps telling me not to worry, just take one day at a time. I say OK, then worry about worrying.

11/09/2007
6:00 PM

Shit is crazy. In the waiting room at surgery today, a super important surgeon dude confused me for another woman who was also waiting on news about a family member. He was this huge guy and he came out with his blue scrubs and a protective facemask thing and a hair net. When we figured out he was talking about the boy with back surgery, not Matt, we took huge breaths of relief. Mark was the kid whose surgery had COMPLICATIONS. Matt was the one who REALLY TOOK A BLOW—doc's words. When he finally figured out who was who, the doc explained how he had sliced open Matt's forehead and glued millimeter-sized pieces of titanium using epoxy to fix his fractured forehead, eye socket and nose. He told us there would be a slight scar from here—he pointed to one ear, and then traced his finger over the front of his head to the other ear—to there. It made me want to puke. The surgeon dude seemed relieved it was over. Is that a good sign? It's all so messed up, but I can't help thinking about the surgeon's life, like if he's married with kids, or like, what does he do for fun? I just have this thing here at the trauma center where I want everyone to love me. If they love me then they'll love Matt and then Matt will be OK. For them to love me I have to pretend I am more confident than I really am, which makes me tired because some days I don't want to wear makeup or smile. I confess it gives me pleasure to imagine that surgeon guy road-biking around Mercer Island at 5 a.m. with his beeper on his hip. His face is super chiseled, but now that I know he's a plastic surgeon I wonder if he's had any plastic surgery done? And what kind of car does he drive? Is his wife a trophy wife or more Type A, like him? Is she the type who peels back a person's face like that, and if so, do they sit around at dinner talking about it? I wonder if he'll remember us when we come back to get the stitches removed. I need to smile more, so he remembers me.

11/10/2007
1:00 AM

There's tons of medical stuff to report but what I want to say is how tonight my girlfriends came by with tequila liquerettes and a lime. They told me how they stole a saltshaker from the cafeteria in the basement. We took tequila shots behind the green vinyl curtain in the ICU. *Hum* went the machines and I finally brushed my hair. I could tell my mother wanted to slap me when I showed up at her house buzzed. Her lips were all pursed and she wanted to MANAGE me and say, where have you been, but she didn't. She DID say, "Joanna is his mother but you are his wife, which means you have power of attorney and more." I know it's true he's going home to me, not her, but she's been so helpful. I mean, it's her son! Tonight, Joanna told me to quit being a "Wilting Lily." The thought of Joanna moving in to help with my husband, her grown son, makes me absolutely ill. My mom tells me our friends and family fundraised for home improvements so that our unfinished house projects will all be wrapped up in time for when Matt comes home. I felt bad that I wasn't excited when she told me. I think maybe friends and family want to be able to do something, so this feels good for them. The thought of Matt coming home to rest among finished projects gives everyone cheer, I guess. The only thing I really want to say about my mom is that she is a kind woman, a loving human being. It's hard to stay at her house and be a good daughter and mother and wife though, and I just really wish this hadn't happened so we don't have to yell at each other when we disagree about dumb crap, like what to watch on TV. She did give me this great book to read about brain trauma and she's really good about making the situation feel less bad by illuminating other worse ones out there. She's always been good with comparisons like that. And she points out the small blessings, which I mean it, I appreciate: the rare good parking spots at Harborview; Lizzie's wonderful kindergarten teacher who doesn't report her tardiness; how we keep getting the BEST doctors and how she has lawyer friends, doctor friends, psychiatrist friends, who can help us. She's really confident we will all be fine, especially because Matt is strong and smart and young and he wants to get better, she can just feel it. I feel like my head is a beehive and words are bees buzzing.

11/11/2007
9:00 PM

Today I was driving my car when I realized I have not yet had a good cry, not even a tear. That's weird, right? I DO understand that my life has been annihilated with ambiguity. I DO take time-outs in the cold cement hospital staircase where I try and weep, I do. When I drive I'm always super careful because, especially now, I just can't die. Today though, my eyes went all blurry and my wipers were not doing the trick, so I pulled over on 21st Ave alongside an empty Metro bus terminal where groups of people sat waiting under the shelter. I let the engine idle. My head collapsed on the steering wheel. Norah Jones was singing on the radio, singing to the Lord about being humbled, which made me just completely choke on my own snot. I guess it's true what Amy says—I'll be eating lots of shit sandwiches here to come. When the city bus came I was still parked in its spot and the driver honked, but I didn't care. I just used my sleeve to wipe the snot from my nose. The driver was pissed and tapped on the window and called me Lady. The rain was coming down sideways (Teddy had said that when he called me—he said Matt's cheekbones were "sideways" . . . I hate that word, "sideways") and the downpour smacked the windows. I sorta wanted to make a scene, like tell him, Hey MISTER, back off this LADY, but since I'm not a total wingnut (yet) I just moved the car. Then I called my mom, who told me I was unfreezing and that they've all been waiting for me to feel it. Waiting for me to feel it? How could I not be feeling it? I don't want for people to be talking about me needing to cry or feel it! I just want my husband back the way he should be, and I want to hide behind being a young pretty mom who has a cute house in a cul-de-sac by the community pool. Ugh! Anyways, I totally wiped my tears and snot with my sleeve and told my mom I'd talk to her later, right after I went to Old Navy. Then she gave me a little guilt trip saying, Come home, let me make you dinner, your daughter needs you, she's been crying for her daddy. This did me in so of course I made a turn to head toward my parents' place, where I had to deal with Lizzie.

◆ ◆ ◆

I became pregnant the spring after our wedding. Matt pretended to be grouchy about it, joking that he thought we needed more time to practice. We lost the baby early and that was disappointing, but in the fall, when I began teaching Spanish classes to little kids, I was pregnant again. During labor Matt sang to me. He rubbed my back. He was an excellent coach. When it came time to push, he cried, I mean really cried. He cut the cord and delivered the news to our families who had waited in the hospital overnight. Later, my mom would describe to me how he'd wept, how he'd wiped his face and said, "We have a perfect baby girl and her name is Elizabeth."

When Lizzie was three months old we took our first trip to the Midwest for a family reunion at the cottage in

Northern Michigan. Far from the hustle of any city, Matt prepared his famous slow-cooked baby back ribs. Earlier, the men in my family had joked about Matt's acumen for anything besides swinging an axe or building a fire, but they didn't have much to say when they were washing down left-over pulled pork sandwiches with Miller Lights on the dock the next day. My uncles and cousins said marriage-affirming stuff like, "Better keep this guy," and, "Not bad, son." One afternoon, Matt took the Sunfish, a trim sailboat, out to the lake by himself. I was thinking, *Oh boy, I hope he brought a life jacket*. I watched from the deck as he shrunk into a pinprick-sized silhouette across the horizon. The after-noon progressed and the weather was picking up. The wind whipped the waves into small peaks. Had he brought a life jacket? When would he be back?

My cousin and I suntanned on a blue-and-white inner tube tied to the dock. "All the men in my town sell mort-gages," she said, flipping to her backside. "Maybe I need to move to the Northwest to meet a *real* man."

I smiled, thinking about how yesterday Matt had joined my aunt and uncle for a speedboat ride early morning, how he had gotten up on a slalom ski on his first try. I left to check on Lizzie, who had been napping in her portable crib. I jiggled her on my chest showing her off to my family when my dad got out the binoculars and stood alert on the deck.

"Uh-oh," he said. "He's down."

All the men took turns behind the binoculars as my dad primed the pump to fire up the Whaler for a rescue. The til-ler, he could see from the binoculars, had busted. Matt was drifting against the tide, far away from shore. In bed that night I hissed at Matt, saying something like, "You could have ended up in the middle of the lake!" I lectured him on the reason they called it Black Lake, on the depth that makes it so dark—what if he had become tired, or worse, what if a storm had come through? Why did he always have to do risky stuff? Did he think he was invincible?

"Nah," he said. "I knew it'd be fine."

I loathed airplane flights when I became a mother, so for travel I would take half a Xanax and order a glass of white wine. Matt always bristled once the drugs kicked in. He told me managing the baby on a plane was a two-parent job.

"Since when?" I would say, pointing to my leaking breasts.

Matt could be gently patriarchal sometimes and his ideas were pretty good, but other times we fought over technicalities. Lizzie had severe colic and would scream roundtrip. Matt was horrified to face stares and tongue clicks as he juggled her up and down the aisle for four hours while I became drowsy. My rationale was, if I was the one who managed the daily drudgery of food prep and clothes cleaning and baby care, I *deserved* a minute to kick back.

We were young like that. I smirked when he wagged his finger and said things like, "That's the last time you take one of those."

It was naïve of us to become so surprised at our parents' conditionality when it came to our babies. It wasn't that they didn't adore our children, but he and I would talk about it with curiosity and a gentle disdain. Why did it seem like they were more interested in relationships with us as adults than with their grandkids? I remember hearing myself weakly defend my parents, saying well, but, they are still working. It stung watching my friends' parents volunteer to

babysit. Joanna wanted all of her son and my mom grew irritable when I wouldn't commit to a mother-daughter lunch
date. This dynamic became even harder when Matt was in
long-term rehabilitation after the accident. I wondered why
our mothers expected so much of us, when it wasn't recipro-
cated the way we needed.

Men are different. They seem to get a pass, which is unfair. Once, my dad was on the same flight on a trip home as
us, probably Michigan again. He was seated a dozen rows
ahead. We were the family with a busy toddler and a fussy
infant, disrupting the flight for a solid four hours. My dad
kept his head in a book, which made me think he was acting
like he didn't know us. I had to rearrange my ideas of what
family closeness meant and stop wishing for things that
wouldn't happen the way I had imagined.

On another flight, I was seated with both children as we
waited on the tarmac for an hour. Matt had a seat in front
of us. It could have appeared as though I was a single parent
if you weren't paying attention. Our chaotic presence must
have given the woman seated to our left great anxiety, for it
wasn't long into being in the air when she shushed me and
the children. Before she shushed me, she rolled her eyes and
sighed—loudly. I am sure Isaac had been doing his bouncy
one-year-old thing. Lizzie had this loud preschool-age-girl
voice, and I could understand how this could be grating, but
this is not the story of a mother neglecting her children. I
entertained. I soothed. I read. Matt turned his body when
he heard the mean lady's passive-aggressive admonishing.
He unbuckled his seat belt and maneuvered his torso so he
was facing her. He stretched out his long pointer finger at
her face.

He said, "That's my family you're talking about."

She quieted down and he traded me spots. I took the Xanax. I ordered the wine.

My brother was marrying a woman from Baltimore, so we booked flights on our credit card and were off traveling again. After the wedding, my parents drove us to Virginia in their rented car. Matt and I rode in the backseat like teenagers. Lizzie had a small mole that would bleed, which we learned was called a hemangioma. It was the size of a pinprick and it was on her forehead. When it got scraped, it bled and we kept a cloth on her forehead. It didn't hurt her, but the amount of blood was shocking and it stressed us all out. She cried extra hard in her car seat that trip. My mom reminded me how in the '70s my bed was a dresser drawer. My dad urged us to remove our fussy one-year-old from her car seat and put her on our laps.

"For crying out loud, nothing's going to happen," he said.

I would have taken her out, but Matt said no way. He told me later, "Just because nothing bad happened to you when you were a baby, doesn't mean something bad can't happen."

My parents' friends invited us to stay in their home in a suburb outside DC. Marianne collected Beanie Babies and went gaga over our real, live doll baby. She didn't care at all when Lizzie bumped a glass angel figurine from a shelf and it shattered. "It's OK," Marianne whispered. "I have lots more."

Lizzie went to bed in her portable crib and woke up with her blonde wispy bangs crusted over with blood. It seeped through the bandage and we plowed through Marianne's box of Band-Aids. The bleeding didn't hurt her, and she was calm as the three of us strolled past the Lincoln Memorial and the Library of Congress at the Capitol. We had an easy picnic along the grassy strip between the driving paths. But she bled and it was worse and longer than the other times and red streaks ran down her face.

A stranger said, "What are you waiting for? Take that baby to the ER!"

They performed a small operation to cauterize the wound and five hours later we were ready to go back to Marianne's house in the suburb. I remember Matt's surprise, how he kept saying, "Jeez, my mom might be a nut, but if her grand-daughter was bleeding, at least she'd offer to help." Where had my parents been all day? And why did I crave their help so badly? Naïve as I may have been to have expected our parents—especially my mom—to offer hands-on support, it was unsettling to come to terms with my role as a full-time caregiver. Would I always be this exhausted?

Back home, we scheduled for Lizzie to have a second procedure at Children's Hospital. It was routine, they said. She'd be in and out. We hoped this time it would be a pro-fessional job and the bleeding would stop for good. Matt held her bitty shoulders down on the white crinkly paper as they cauterized the hemangioma in a severe way so it never came back. I didn't go. Afterward, Matt described how she had looked at him and asked, "Why, Daddy?" I asked him what he told her and he said, "I told her it was going to be fine. I told her I'd protect her."

Living through the days after Matt's accident was like sur-rendering to a violent ocean, getting pounded by wave after wave. I clenched my stomach in preparation for something I didn't understand.

As for the children, it was just easier to tell them their daddy was at work, which sufficed for a few days. Once we knew Matt was certain to live, my parents and Joanna and I agreed to tell the kids he was sick at the hospital. When Lizzie asked after her daddy I lied, saying he was OK and would be home soon. I wanted to put off the experience for as long as possible. We did little simple things instead, like feed seagulls French fries from Ivar's at Pier 54. One day we were driving and singing along to the *Curious George* soundtrack when Lizzie told me to turn it off. It was a week or so after the accident and we were living at my parents' house full time. I always drove them to school in the mornings, but I spent most afternoons and evenings at the hospital. Isaac hurled a juice box at my head, maybe a reaction to the fresh silence, I can't say.

"I want to see Daddy," Lizzie said.

I looked at her in the rearview mirror. Her rosebud lips were turned down and her face was drawn. We parked in my parents' driveway and I unbuckled them from their car seats and told her not tonight. She began to cry.

"I want to see my daddy! I want to go home!"

Isaac began to cry. I put him down and looked at my mom, who had come outside to greet us. She took my hand, and his. The pressure of holding my own grief and anxiety in check was becoming unbearable and I felt myself for a second wish *I* was the one in a medical coma. *How quiet for him*, I thought, *how calm*. I screamed at my two young children. I may have even told them to shut up. My mom led me into her room after we sat the kids down for a snack. She said something about how kids know when their parents lie. She used my name for emphasis and the honesty in the exchange felt heavy-handed, which pissed me off, and also made me tremble. I was quick to be pissed in those days, quick to tremble. It was effort trying to unclench the clench that lived in the pits of my lower abdomen. I know now that the blood vessels in my viscera were constricting to make more blood so that my muscles could prepare to respond with physical action. This was my body's natural defense against the threat of the trauma. My muscle tone felt altered the very moment I saw Matt's condition and realized it was the beginning of a new, unwelcome life experience. More symptoms would develop over time, but for now, it was this tightness in the belly. It was like I was always waiting for someone to tell me worse news. I couldn't relax.

My mom lectured me on how the kids needed me at dinner and for bedtime and that Matt was in good hands.

"OK, I'll take them," I told her, grabbing my coat. "But you're coming with."

We left Isaac with my dad. He could feed him hotdogs and peas. I gathered up a blanket and buckled Lizzie in. Lizzie wore her My Little Pony pj's and we listened to Jack Johnson sing a song about recycling. I could see in my periphery how my mom was folding and unfolding her hands on her lap. We parked in the underground garage. It was dark and cold and I had an idea. I told Lizzie, "Daddy is sleeping because it's nighttime. I'm going to give Gamma these few things for Daddy and you and Mimi can stay here, OK?" She nodded, like it was the simplest thing.

Walking toward the entrance, I marveled over the raw honesty of children. It seemed she was OK with the plan because somehow she knew it was a first step—like my responding to her request meant everything would be fine.

I squirted antibacterial gel into my palm at the first desk I came to. That scent, the cold, clear gel liquid, has forever seeped into my conscious; every time I use it or smell it on someone else, I think not of hospitals directly, but of emergency vehicles, or intracranial pressure monitors, or the clank of metal wheels rolling portable beds with patients down the hall.

I took the elevator to floor three. I kissed his cheek and rearranged his hospital bed pillow. He was mute, his blackened eyes glued shut with crusted pus. The crook of his arm where he'd been poked for IVs was yellowing. This had to be a quick trip. Joanna was somewhere, maybe getting coffee in the basement cafeteria. I didn't text her. Sometimes, I didn't want an update from his mother, upbeat as she always tried to be. I'd see her later anyways, at my parents' house where she was also staying. I took the gift Matt's cousin had delivered and made my way to the elevator.

"Here," I said, giving Lizzie the white teddy bear. "Daddy wants you to have this."

Lizzie nestled into the white stuffed bear. It came with a felt rose and a chocolate bar. She snuggled under her cozy blanket and fell asleep on the way home.

A week or so later I would take them both to see him in his new room post-surgery. One of his eyelids was opened a crack and the IVs had been removed. We grown-ups were all saying how great he looked, how wonderful he was recovering, but that was amongst ourselves, his witnesses and cheerleaders. I can't imagine the shock it must have been for the small children. Lizzie went to reach for her daddy's hand and Isaac stayed on my lap sucking his shirt. Children this age do not ask detailed questions, or ours didn't. Matt wasn't saying much and we didn't stay long. The message was simple: he is ill, but he is healing.

I'm OK with Seattle's county trauma hospital not spending tax dollars on remodels to accommodate visitors. Nothing about that place is snazzy. It is good to spend the money on surgery and equipment and nurse staff. The enormity of the buildings and the stacks of floors and elevators and cement stairways provided enough entertainment for the children when I'd take them to visit in subsequent afternoons. When Matt finally moved to rehab, we discovered the "family room" where they had couches and a TV and coloring books and a foosball table. This is where our friends would visit amongst themselves if Matt was resting, and where Isaac would bounce around shouting, "I'll win you!" to his sister.

Matt's first roommate at the hospital was a guy named Chit. He was an older man from Idaho who, if his young girlfriend could be trusted, had raced cars with Evel Knievel in the '80s. Chit had had a tree accident too, only his accident wasn't as much of an assault as it was a true slip-and-fall. He had a broken pelvis and his jaw was wired shut, but his head was fine. His girlfriend interpreted his grunting.

"He likes Matt," she told me.

"How can you tell?" I asked her.

"You all seem so nice. I just know it. They'd have a lot to talk about—you know, logger stuff," she said.

On floor five with Chit, Matt had the window side. Something about being able to see the crows on the wire soothed me. The evening sky was always jewel-toned and beyond the gray cladding of skyscrapers we could see a slice of the snow-peaked Olympic mountains. Matt was still mute after surgery, but the NG tubes were gone. His face reminded me of rotting fruit, eyelids like new plums. His crumpled skull was smoothed out and his face had features again.

As the days wore on, Chit's young girlfriend and I shared good news, things like when Nurse Liz put a pen in Matt's hand and he signed his own initials. We grew excited together when our men swallowed applesauce. She celebrated with me when the director of rehabilitation decided Matt was a solid candidate for inpatient rehab. (The alternative to inpatient rehab is going home too soon, or worse, being referred to a nursing facility.) At the trauma hospital, people know what they're doing. There are no small concussions. It is filled with the confidence of expensive research. It has the aura of hope, fed by the constant chorus of nurses and doctors who in your dreams you mistake for angels.

When Chit's kind girlfriend packed his stuff up one afternoon and said their goodbyes, I was shocked. I wasn't ready for them to go. That's when I learned just how fast things move at Harborview.

Matt's next roommate was Rod, flown in from Alaska after his head made contact with an iron stove. He'd crushed his skull so bad he needed a new one. Daily he offered to remove his helmet to show me the soft spot on his left temporal lobe, and daily I said no thank you. He was one of these guys I saw out front at the hospital entrance in his issued hospital pajamas, smoking with the street guys. He seemed more conscious than Chit or Matt, flipping through cable channels and making commentary. I found out it wasn't his first trip to Harborview. Only the Oxycodone drip quieted him down. Rod seemed to be doing well, which made me feel depressed.

"How about them Seahawks?" he said loudly.

I was preoccupied with Matt's thrashing underneath wrist restraints, but not too busy to become short with Rod.

"Can you turn that down?" I hissed.

We'd been instructed to keep lights low, sounds to a minimum. No visitors but family.

"For a price, sweetheart, or a beer." He winked. "I won't tell," he said. Wink, wink.

I rolled my eyes and huffed a little, calling for the nurse so I could ask when we could switch rooms. I learned there would be no switching.

It was in the room with Rod that I undressed and laid next to my husband in his hospital bed. Up until this point his body had been too fragile and there had been too many tubes, too many specialists. I wanted to feel his skin against mine. I knew it couldn't hurt. I positioned the curtain between Matt and Rod so I could feel as though I had a little privacy. I undressed into the essentials: bra, underwear, socks. Matt had zero notion as I squeezed myself alongside him. He's not a small guy and made no effort to move over. It is painful to relive this ten years later. But Rod. He stuck up for me when the nurse came in and clucked at me a little.

"You're not supposed to get in bed with post-op patients," she said.

Rod piped up, as though he had been waiting for the chance to defend us all.

"Aw, give the little lady a break—she's just trying to get it on with her man!"

I warmed to Rod after that. I became patient with him, even watching a little football and grabbing him some ice water. I wasn't necessarily sad to see him go, but I was grateful he had provided me with some necessary comfort.

Next was Jake, a seventeen-year-old kid from Hoquiam, a small coastal town three hours' drive away. He'd been working at the dock for the Port of Grays Harbor when he was struck by a log. It was unclear what he did for work exactly; it had something to do with loading and unloading logs. Another occupational injury resulting from manual labor. Fresh inside the denial of our reality, it surprised me to hear Jake and his family talk about the insurance they were owed, like that was the most important thing. We learned later, and I can't remember from whom, how he'd been struck on the left side of his head by one of the logs and lost nearly all hearing. His family was *excited* about the twenty thousand dollars he would be awarded from Workers' Compensation, the same industrial insurance who would be taking care of Matt's bills. He could get a new truck, he kept saying. His was a "closed" head injury, meaning there would not be surgery. His appearance gave off the impression he was fine, until he wasn't. He talked constantly about petty things. He took seven showers a day. He irritated staff when he wandered the facility shirtless. I'm sure they didn't care for his family, either.

"Don't you think the Somali orderlies ought to *at least* speak English?" whispered his mom.

"I know, right? Like when you ask them something and they just nod . . . it's so annoying," his sister said.

His girlfriend chimed in: "Don't you think we should hide his guns before he comes home?"

Matt's doctor was a teeny Chinese woman I wanted to take home with me. She must have understood how this particular roommate exchange made me teeter on the edge when she saw me sit in a chair with my head in my hands. She touched my shoulder and asked if I was OK. I nodded, bleary-eyed. How could I tell her I was wondering how this redneck kid could be doing so well while my loving husband struggled swallowing food? I hated myself for the way I felt.

"Please don't panic," she said. "That boy came in here with problems. You are a strong family and your husband meets all the factors for a solid recovery: he's young, drug-free, smart, and has a great support system. Most of all, he wants to get better. Everyone here can see that."

I wanted to tell her I wasn't strong. I wanted to cry on her shoulder. I wanted her to tell me something else, something quantifiable, like, "In three months he will be back to normal."

After Jake was Thuhong, who also went by Rick. He barely made this list. He called himself *half-a-hippie* because for his surgery they shaved the left half of his long hair. His semicircle scar spanned the right side of his skull. Matt didn't think Rick's *half-a-hippie* joke was funny: he was pained about his own strange haircut. For surgery, he'd been buzzed only up to the point in his hairline in which they needed to make an incision.

"Why didn't they just finish the whole job?" he moaned, gingerly fingering the bloody scabs surrounding the blue staples sewn from ear to ear. "I look like a Hari Krishna."

We learned Rick had been living in Port Townsend as a deckhand when he fell down three flights of stairs at a bar. I wanted to ask him if it was the popular bar in that Victorian on Main Street downtown. Rick liked to talk about himself: I learned he was a competitive crossword puzzle gamer and in his former life had been a mathematics professor. I wondered how he came to become a deckhand in a small port town. Was alcoholism at the root of all this injury? I always raced to rehab after dropping the kids at school, and I was surprised the day I came and Rick was gone. He'd had his surgery and insurance had run out. Like Rod, Rick never had any visitors. Which makes you wonder, who picked them up? Where did they go?

Second to last was a young man named Jon. He'd suffered a brain aneurism while riding a bike in Seattle. His job was working as a tech at a bike store in Seattle, and like Jake and Rod and Rick, he was talkative, but nothing he said was serious.

"I just can't wait to get back to the shop," he kept saying. Like nothing had happened.

The way these men appeared normal triggered nausea and that stomach clench. Jon was in Matt's speech therapy group and did all the assignments. Matt's notebook was blank. That was because Matt could not read the newspaper. He could not remember the assigned tasks. And yet Jon's mother was so worried. She told me this wasn't Jon's first time. There it was again. A second time.

"There was an incident with wrestling and concrete," she told me.

When Jon wasn't reading the paper, or talking on his cell phone, he slept. He slept *a lot*. I learned he had a girlfriend who broke up with him when she heard the news. Jon kept asking about her.

"I always thought she was a floozy," his mom said when Jon was in a physical therapy session. I nodded. I brought her coffee. We shared magazines.

The last roommate before Matt's release was a black homeless Vietnam veteran named Michael. I wasn't there when police brought him in cuffed and high, but Matt was talking by then and filled me in. Michael, he said, had been severely beaten and left for dead under the James Street overpass. His belongings had fit in one green duffel bag. At night, he messed with the mechanics of the hospital bed, making it hard for Matt to get rest. Selection for inpatient rehab is a handpicked process, so when Michael took off without sign-off paperwork, the staff was ticked. The sudden departure left Matt ornery—he was certain inside Michael's green duffel was his own shaving cream and razor.

"I helped him turn off that annoying hospital bed alarm, and he swipes my stuff?"

I told him not to worry; we'd get him some more.

"Yeah, but that's not the point. He took my stuff."

I was having a hard time locating *the point* to any of this crazy shit. I never stopped thinking about those guys after we went home. I still think about them. Every time I see someone with one of those scars like Rick I want to ask them how it was for them, what they remember.

◆ ◆ ◆

(a letter)

Hey.

Hey, remember when you borrowed your cousin's Glock? "It's a people killer," you said. "No one should have one of these, especially not cops." I liked how you never wanted to hurt anyone. You told me the story of how one time with your cousin Billy from Wyoming, you'd refused to finish off a deer you guys had accidentally hit driving in the dark. You had nightmares watching Billy bludgeon it to death with a mallet. We parked on a dirt road and made out in your cherry-red Forerunner. I asked a million questions about the gun: How far do the bullets shoot? Was this your first time? Do the Kishpaugh boys regularly share artillery? How do we know we weren't going to shoot a passerby? You told me to calm down. You said, "Hey, I got this—OK?" You positioned the empty Coke can atop a stump, and filled the quiet air with a tale:

"So I'm taking a dip in the Willamette at Lando's family farm, right? I'm putting on my clothes after jumping in the river when I hear this noise. It sounds like someone crying. A little kid. I run through the thickets following the sound. I yell and yell, 'Where are you?' but whoever it was kept yelling, 'Help! Help!' in this pathetic voice. I couldn't figure out where the sounds were coming from, so I yell for the kid to stay where he was. I yell, 'I'm coming!' and leap over logs and tear through brush."

You laughed and walked back from the Coke can and drew forth a box of bullets from the Forerunner.

"So I get to a clearing in the woods, and by now I'm panting and sweaty and about half mile from the farm. I've been yelling for help all this time and all of a sudden I hear footsteps behind me."

You loaded the Glock and pointed to the safety. You said, "So you have to lift this up before shooting—" and I said, "Finish the story! What happened to the kid?"

You sat the gun down on the truck's bed and folded your arms across your chest.

"So I came into a clearing and there was this peacock. A peacock with its feathers all splayed out like a rainbow. I stopped for a second to check it out then passed the bird. So I'm three hundred yards into the brush yelling for the kid to stay where he is when I hear that same 'Help!' sound right behind me. I turn around and the peacock is flexing his neck, screaming like a little kid. Did you know peacocks make that noise? 'Help! Help!'"

You laughed at yourself, how you imitated the noise. I teased you, said you went on a mission for nothing. I said, "Just so you know, I'm no marksman." I'd been noticing small children everywhere. I thought you were a nice man to jump through thickets to save a small child, even if it was only a peacock. With our contrasting skin and hair, we'd make pretty babies. I cocked the Glock, took aim and fired. Remember how the tin blasted the air? You could hardly believe my good aim. You secured the safety and lit a cigarette. I blushed and blamed it on beginner's luck. But you thought it was cool, when you saw it up close, the battered Coke can I'd smoked in the distance.

◆ ◆ ◆

11/18/2007
3:00 PM

I'm so not ready for the real world yet—and yet I'm getting real
sick of this place. It does feel safe to be around professionals,
and I know it's good Dr. Singh called the Centers for Disease
Control to run tests for Matt's peaked temperatures and oddly
swollen hands that to me look like oven mitts, but Jesus, it's
his birthday—can't the guy catch a teeny little break? His room
is all hush-hush now that visitors have left. His birthday gifts,
which he couldn't care less about and I don't blame him, are
a pair of Puma sneakers, a track suit (size medium b/c he's lost
forty pounds), and a pair of Ray-Ban aviator-style sunglasses
I chose that are cool as shit. Someone from his work came by
with some outdoorsy-type magazines so I stuck them on the
windowsill. I didn't really want to watch the anesthesiologist
collect cerebrospinal fluid for a spinal tap, so I left to get fresh
air. They told me he is in good hands, and Joanna is supposed to
be here soon. My mom keeps telling me my job is the kids, and
I need to rest and eat, so I can take care of them. I feel so useless
here. I'm gonna go take a walk.

11/18/2007
8:00 PM

Oh my fucking God! That anesthesiologist is SUCH a CUNT!
She was marking up iodine on Matt's back when I got back
from walking around on the campus at Seattle U. Matt didn't
ask where I'd been and Joanna wasn't there. This needle was

big, like for an epidural. Matt grimaced and she rolled her eyes like he was the biggest pain in her ass! She needed him to relax, she kept saying. And he kept worming around, arching his back, saying wait, I'm not ready. She kept saying fuck and goddammit, and I'm thinking, is this JERK for real swearing at my husband? How long had she been on the clock? She's not even supposed to be here, she says, but her colleague got sick. So then she tells these insipid jokes, and Matt beats her to the punch line, and I want to kiss him because he's no dummy. It went like this:

ANESTHESIOLOGIST JERK: Which fish can perform operations?

MATT: A sturgeon.

ME: Ha!

She didn't even give Matt credit or act impressed, she just upped her ante with the next joke, one of those trick questions no one ever gets right and I'm over here thinking, Oh, this CUNT must want trouble.

ANESTHESIOLOGIST JERK: So two kippers are hanging out. The first kipper says to the second kipper, "Smoking's bad for you." What does the second kipper say back?

MATT: Hmmmm . . .

ANESTHESIOLOGIST JERK: Second kipper says back, "It's OK, I've been cured."

ME (thinking): I'm gonna kill your face.

I'M SO SURE! She didn't even give him a chance to think! He totally winced when the needle entered the small of his back. Then she has the gall to smile (with her lips closed) and say to me, When this is all over he needs to buy you a big fat diamond ring, as she packs away her kit. When this is over. When will that be? I hate her for reminding me how attached I am to our cute married-with-kids life. I DO want to think about buying new shiny gems and getting estimates for finishing the deck and shopping the Nordstrom Half-Yearly sale for Lizzie's clothes. Isaac will need preschool soon and I'll need to look for work, maybe even full-time. Ugh! My mom keeps telling me how Matt will have challenges. I hate it when she's honest, but it's OK—I have tons of ideas for what he can do when he gets better: a landscaping business (white pickup, high-end tools); urban arborist consulting (a chip truck, new saws); real estate (a suit and tie?). My dad already told me they were good for a loan if he needs to quit tree work. Everyone knows Matt is competent and can do anything he puts his mind to. Last night I told Hannah on the phone how I thought things might actually be BETTER than they were before. Like maybe he'll be more sensitive, more careful. After the spinal tap I went to floor two to write my daily status update on the blog we set up. I kept out the part about the foot-long needle and the overtired hospital staff. I wrote: "Happy birthday to Matt! Surgery went smooth. He is talking, walking and on the road to recovery." What a beautiful little liar I have become. Ugh. When I got back to the room, his roommate Jake from Hoquiam was talking about Matt as though he wasn't in the room. Jake had his shirt off and was flexing in the mirror after a shower, his third for the day. "They keep poking that poor guy," he said, thumbing at his squat mother in Matt's direction. "If they could just stop with the poking, we'd all be fine." Ugh. Get me the eff out of here!

11/20/2007
5:00 AM

My sister-in-law yelled at me the other day. She told me I needed to let her make a spreadsheet. I'm having a hard time organizing the kids. I guess I've been a real pill, as my Gammie would say. I'm not good at letting people help me. Or maybe I just don't know how or what to delegate, because I'm in shock? But Malia works at Microsoft and is kind of a ball-buster so I should probably trust her. It does feel as though she's got my back. So I said OK. I hope she doesn't fuck up and leave my five-year-old alone at the bus stop. Jesus!

12/01/2007
8:00 AM

Yesterday Matt failed the counting change test. I am not always there for everything, but I was there for that. I also heard a depressing conversation between Matt and the staff speech therapist where he confessed he was BRAIN DAMAGED (his words). He said it so matter-of-fact—like that was it, we're done here. The speech pathologist saw the horrified look on my face and found me later and told me how right now, there is not much flexibility in his thinking, but try not to be too alarmed. Recovery for healthy patients is usually exponential. The word exponential makes me think of the math graph from 7th grade. Up and up on the y-axis. Oh, I see, he's on the up and up, like my mom always says. I asked the speech lady if she'd read Lee

Woodruff's book, *In an Instant: A Family's Journey of Love and Healing*. My mom gave me the book and I devoured it in one sitting. Her response kinda pissed me off. She said how that book focuses on the immediate nature of the injury. How it's all about rehab. How MY hard work will be at home in the coming years. Hold on just a second. Years? Is this a joke? Ludicrous. He is thirty-two, I mean thirty-three. An Oregonian. A woodsman. My champion. A father. Maybe this lady just doesn't like me because she saw me accidentally throw a Nerf football in Matt's face during physical therapy. Anyways, the good news is they are getting ready to release him. The next step is all these tests, like make a map and buy groceries and cook food. Should be fun, ha ha!

◆ ◆ ◆

Candace and Mary were part of the OT rehab crew. OT stands for Occupational Therapist. A patient on a neurological inpatient rehab unit must be able to eat, feed, and dress independently, before they are released from rehab for home. The expectation is not getting the patient back to *normal*—the idea is for a patient to be safe unto himself. There would be months of outpatient sessions scheduled, sometimes three appointments at three different times at three different locations, all on one day. But before all that, doctors must be satisfied with the answers to these basic questions before allowing the patient to leave rehab: Will the patient become lost? Can the patient manage money? What about hygiene—are they capable of taking care of themselves?

For Matt, the rehab docs had already determined he wouldn't need a nursing facility, but he still needed to check off the basics. For me, I wished we could stay longer, wait a bit more. I wanted the comfort of our home, and my heart was hopeful about a full recovery, but I was unsure how I would handle the new responsibilities. To comfort myself, I turned to our young children every night. I stroked their sweet cheeks while they were sleeping and rolled into their soft bodies. I can do this, I thought. I will.

It was another bone-chilling day where all the layers plus the fleece didn't do the trick. Candace reminded Matt to grab the list he'd made for the trip to the store. Mary gave him a ten spot. Matt understood he was supposed to follow a map he'd drawn; he was to lead us out of the hospital, around the block, and back again. He took us down the elevator to the lobby. He pressed the crosswalk button and we waited. Groupings of leaves whirled around us as gusts of freezing wind smashed our faces.

Those cute OT girls (they seemed like girls to me) didn't know my husband was once a helicopter pilot and that we used to call him a human compass. We continued toward Broadway and circled back around, making a square. Easy. Mary peered over his shoulder at the map. He unfolded it and handed it to her.

She said, "Did we go the route you planned, Matt?"

He shrugged and asked if it was time to go back yet.

Mary said, very gently, "You're going to take us shopping now, right?"

The nearest market was on the ground floor of one of these spanking new condos for young executives. Mary reminded him to take a hand basket. He strolled through the aisles, limping along. He picked up random items here and there and held them against the light, squinting. The items rang up at $13.25—slightly over budget. He unfolded his crumpled ten and motioned to me with his hands.

He said, "Let me have your debit card."

Candace giggled. "Gosh," she said.

Mary said, "He is so clever."

They were both pretty young. Matt weaved us through a sea of homeless men on our way back toward Harborview where in a special room with a stove he melted butter in a pan he used to fry an egg. He sliced cheese and boiled a chicken breast. Mary cut through the meat to test its doneness and Matt had a bite, then threw it all away.

"Can I go to my room now?" he said.

To get a break from the trauma center, I would walk downhill toward the Seattle University campus where I could revel in the beauty of the Chapel of St. Ignatius. I would kick up leaves on Broadway worrying over the homeless who I was sure had suffered street violence–related concussions. The underbellies of leaf piles look like squished grape stains. This time of year, if we were home and not stuck living in my parents' basement, Matt would be stoking a fire and I would be simmering a roast in the Crockpot. We would be talking about plans for Thanksgiving and how the inches of rain translated to snow for skiing.

I noticed students in button-down shirts carrying heavy backpacks because paying attention to the beauty of youth calmed me. I liked to go around three in the afternoon so that when I left, it was dusk. I would follow the lowering orange sun back up the hill, never hurrying, though

I knew people were waiting. This was my break time, my alone time with a higher power in a serene spot. The chaos of the city trauma center could wait. I would approach the walkway leading to the chapel and sit on the cement knee-high bench surrounding the wishing well adjoining the small, modern chapel. I'd give the crisp air a good sniff and let my purse drop to the bench. A few students milled around. They let me be. There weren't coins in the shallow pool, so I wouldn't take one from my purse to use for a wish. The entrance to the chapel had wooden doors the height of the ceiling with large cutouts of oblong holes that looked like large eggs had been fired through. I'd crack the door open and walk past the standing baptistery bowl and into the center section where I'd sit on a pew in the east nave. The floor was poured concrete, like the kind I dreamt for my kitchen. Shadows bounced off yellow and blue color fields painted on the back of suspended baffles. I'd kneel at the wooden pew and let the fog settle inside my brain. I'd finally cry—gently, not a sob, but a flow of pent-up feelings racing from my eyes toward some undesignated finish line. I'd allow myself to finally be as sad as I wanted. Here in the quiet, I'd reflect on my new experiences of the unbearably kind gestures of strangers.

Whenever I took Lizzie to her kindergarten class, groups of mothers would ask what they could do. They said they wanted to organize a carpool and bring casseroles, but I didn't know them very well. Lizzie had been in full-day kindergarten for just two months at the time of the accident. I had had all these ideas about how the first year of our first child's schooling would go. To the kind mothers, it was hard for me to say things like, "No, thanks," and "I don't know," when they asked all their questions. Instead, I'd smile and make stuff up and put on my sunglasses and cry in the car.

Lizzie's teacher pulled me aside one afternoon at parent pickup. He loved my daughter and was concerned. He was actually pretty cute and in my despair, I developed a small crush, probably because he had nice muscles and hugged Lizzie a lot and never cared when we were late. He taught her to read. I forgave him when he stared at me and asked if Matt's situation was like the guy from the *Memento* movie. I sort of blinked at him trying to imagine what he was getting at, then I remembered the film's premise about the guy whose short-term memory loss every five minutes was born from a traumatic event. How could I tell him I had zero idea how this all would end? I was in my own movie and it was happening now.

I remember how once he asked me, as childlike as the kids he managed every morning, "Aren't you wondering why me, why now?" I didn't have the heart or conscience or wherewithal to say yes or no. What he was getting at was a sense of awe only outsiders have the privilege of feeling. Another time a sweet nurse mom said, "You will change so much from this experience." She was another person who told me the hard work would be *after* the hospital. I wanted to thank them for their graciousness, but if I opened my mouth nothing came out.

I would leave Lizzie sitting on a carpet scrap with a picture book and drive back to the city to sort through what was growing into impossible levels of bureaucratic shit.

Matt's belongings fit into one cardboard box. He had been at Harborview for forty-two days and I couldn't wait to take him home. In the box: two pairs of sweatpants, travel-sized bottles of saline solution, mini-packets of Neosporin, a stack of handwritten cards, a hardbound *Neurosurgery and You* binder, his rehab-issued green agenda booklet, his ripped arborist clothes, a beat-up leather wallet, and the Bill Bryson book, *A Walk in the Woods*.

We were at a meeting with his rehab team sitting at the end of the table in a tight room with windows overlooking the Sound. It felt like a board meeting I should be preparing coffee for. Matt had had so many helpers in so little time, and most were there: the psychiatrist who had administered multiple tests; the otolaryngologist who had fixed his face; the rehab floor physicians who had managed his post-op care, and the lead vocational therapist.

The doctors reminded him that he wasn't supposed to drive, or drink alcohol for six months. We talked about out-patient meetings at UW he would start up in late January. Where to park, who to contact, what to expect. Mostly they were tight-lipped. We wanted to leave the hospital in time for the holidays, and they wanted us to, too. I was surprised they were OK with this early release. It's like when you have a baby and you want to take him home, and they actually let you, and you're happy but scared. Everything was new like that.

Matt rolled himself around in the office chair like an executive. He pointed to the words on the whiteboard and said, "So, what you're saying is, I have to come back for appointments. After that I go back to work."

It wasn't the first time he had referenced going back to work. It may have been one of the first things he talked about after surgery, after they took out the stents in his nose and he began talking a little. He also had wanted to know how much all this was costing, which would have been charming if he wasn't so off in his estimate. He kept saying to friends and family, "This is setting me back about five grand."

Staff found his positive attitude refreshing and tossed around words like *wherewithal* and *staying power*. It made me wince. He had a scar from ear to ear over his forehead and one eye was still shut and we didn't know the degree to which he had lost sight. He couldn't count change so well. The left side of his face was sunken and he weighed 152 pounds. We had two small children at home waiting for Santa to bring them gifts. I needed a job, but my job needed to be my family.

Adrenaline kicked in as I took the kids' art and family photos from the wall. I looked out the window and said goodbye to my crow friend on the electrical wire. I made Matt three separate therapy appointments and signed him up for a traumatic brain injury support group.

I had these homemade cranberry bread loaves I wanted to deliver to the nurses in the ICU. I tried to hold Matt's hand but he shook it away. I guessed he was kind of pissed about being so hurt.

The charge nurse on floor two said, "I remember you."

The nurse looked at me: "Motorcycle accident, right?"

I shook my head and reminded him about the tree.

"Right, right. Around Halloween, I remember now. The end of trauma season."

That was a thing?

Matt looked around for a place to sit and Eric the nurse gave him a pat on the back, real loving-like.

"You look great, man. Keep doing what you're doing. It's all you."

We took the elevator to the basement where we bought a cup of cafeteria drip coffee. I said something dumb like, "One for the road." The few remaining leaves on the city vine maples were the color of toast. I struggled with the cardboard box in my arms opening the passenger side door for Matt.

As I drove he said, "Slow down." He put his head between his knees and opened the window a crack.

I had been to the house a few times to check out the remodel going on. My dad had led the efforts, cutting, painting and caulking moldings where they had been missing, which was all over the house. He had painted all the kitchen cupboards so they looked bright and clean. A whole crew of Matt's friends finished closing in the car port Matt had begun painting that summer, and a good friend of mine was project manager on the bathroom: new tile, bathtub, toilet, fixtures, lights. They timed it all so they would be done when we got home.

My friend had said, "We want Matt to feel comfortable, so he can relax."

They knew him well. He had a hard time with unfinished projects. He had a hard time with rest. We entered the house and he looked around a little at the updates but made no reaction. I pointed stuff out, like look here at the new swinging door Bob engineered, or check out the water-efficient toilet, but he was just quiet. That was OK. No one expected anyone to gush or be grateful.

There were a dozen helium balloons with $100 bills stuffed inside—so creative! Someone had left homemade cookies on the counter. There was a note from work saying a meal delivery service was planned for Monday. A petite Christmas tree stood naked in the living room corner.

I can't remember where the children were, only that they weren't there when we got home. When they got dropped off, I would instruct them to be quiet, so Daddy could rest. And no jumping on Daddy. This of course would work some days, and not on others. They were five and two and a half. We closed the bedroom door a lot so he could be alone in the dark.

The support of family and friends helped balance out the fear of the unknown. The only thing I wasn't ambiguous about was ambiguity itself. If there had already been confusion, there would only be a lot more ahead. For now, I had friends to thank, people to explain things to. I knew I could never repay them for their generosity.

My heart felt full, like something had bloomed inside.

PART II

Modest split-level '60s homes with large driveways and moderately landscaped yards. A few ornamental trees without leaves strung with Christmas lights. SARAH climbs the front steps to a neighbor's front door. Neighbor MARI opens it and embraces Sarah. Sarah is skinnier than Mari remembers. She enters and smiles, nodding to TIM, Mari's husband, and their three kids who are sitting in the living room. The kids stop everything to hear the grown-ups talk. Mari gives Sarah a long tight hug.

TIM

Do you want some coffee?

Sarah shakes her head. Stays standing. A pause.

SARAH

Thanks for getting the mail.

MARI

Of course. Are you home for good now?

SARAH

Yes, thank God.

Mari makes a motion with her arms toward Sarah and Matt's house.

MARI

There's been a lot of action over there.

Sarah shrugs, smiles weakly—

SARAH

They painted and put in a new tub and sink and put up base-boards. They also finished siding on the carport.

MARI

Was all that OK with you? I mean, was it your decision?

SARAH

My mom and my friend Holly organized it.

TIM

There have been a lot of trucks coming and going.

Sarah nods. Mari and Tim's youngest, eight-year-old IAN, walks into the kitchen. He addresses Sarah, who is now rifling through her large stack of mail.

IAN

Hey, is Matt gonna be blind?

MARI

Ian!

SARAH

It's OK. Um, no, not all the way. A little bit, right here.

(She points to her left eye.)

IAN

We raked the leaves for you.

SARAH

Thanks.

IAN

Will Matt have to wear a patch?

Tim shakes his head. Sarah laughs.

SARAH

He might. Like a pirate, yeah.

TIM

So now, did Matt have brain surgery?

SARAH

It was more like plastic surgery, to repair fractures in his forehead and eye sockets and nose.

TIM

So not brain surgery, like with my dad, where they knifed out the tumor.

MARI

Tim! She just said it was plastic surgery.

TIM

But wasn't there a thing with the brain? Like will he have to relearn how to walk and talk?

SARAH

He can do all that. He's doing awesome, actually. He just needs some rest, I think.

MARI

Let us know if you need anything.

Sarah nods, turns to go.

SARAH

I will, I promise.

Sarah sits on her stoop with the mail in her lap with the winter daytime sun in her face. She glances at the rooftop, at the strung colored Christmas lights. How did those get there? She removes a check from an envelope, another gift from a relative. She looks up to see another couple of neighbors, two women who attend the same church, heading her way. She sniffs the clean air and takes a small bottle from her purse and squirts lotion in her palm.

◆ ◆ ◆

(a letter)

Hey.

Hey, remember how when we were first dating and you invited me to visit you in Northern Idaho? It was the summer after you earned your helicopter license, right? They hired you on with that logging operation and you bought that big blue Ford truck and a trailer to live in since the work was two weeks on, one week off. I drove fast in my red VW Golf blasting Alanis Morissette the whole way. We would get in your pickup with mugs of instant coffee and tear through the forest service road at like 5 a.m.! There was that man they called "The Brain Surgeon," for the reason he wore tank tops in the dead of winter. I had overslept and made us late, so you ripped around the tight bends of the skinny forest road trying to get us all to the site on time. I remember how we picked up The Brain Surgeon on the way there and he said to you, "Hey champ, the lady here wants to get back to your trailer tonight in one piece."

You were the youngest on that crew, weren't you? We arrived and you and the men drank more Folgers. You introduced me to your boss, who invited me inside the double rotor yellow Sikorsky. It was naked and empty, like one of my dad's ship's hulls. For the job that day, the machine would carry one pilot and one copilot: you. The machine carried underslung loads of logs using a remote hook suspended from the belly with a long line. Does that sound right? Am I telling this part OK? You told me how the swath of the double rotor carrying logs made the machine a wobbling teeter-totter. I watched from the ground, imagining you steadying your logbook on your lap as you penciled in data about fuel and mileage. I learned from the guys in the trailer that you were notorious for being the only copilot who never puked. A stomach of steel, they said. Remember how I gushed over the operation while we ate beans inside your trailer? You asked if I'd like to learn how to make tamales. Tomorrow, maybe Alonso's wife could teach me. You said of course we could take a hike after work. I asked if flying was hard and you patted me and said, "Try not to glorify piloting. It's really just like truck driving in the sky."

◆ ◆ ◆

Matt was in pretty bad shape after the hospital; Joanna was correct to be concerned. She'd offered to move in and help out, take a leave of absence from work. She had been so helpful at the hospital I almost said yes, but my mom stopped me, telling me something about how I was the wife and I had to step up. Knowing how Matt felt about his mother's boundaries, I asked myself, what would Matt want? Back then he was wandering from room to room, wondering what had hit him. He was nauseated, sleeping at least sixteen hours a day. The changes in his physicality were a cutthroat loss. As his full-time witness, I identified how he likely wouldn't care what or who was doing the helping—he just wanted the ringing in his ears to cease. I still wanted to be the one to defend him, though.

I took my mom's advice and convinced Joanna I could handle him on my own. I remember she looked at me with this crazed, anxious look in her eye, and who could blame her? I was no nurse. But then during the holidays, things sort of unraveled. Joanna called to give Matt a message: Surprise! She'd bought the kids each one of those huge motorized cars from Toys "R" Us. The size of my disdain over the motorized cars gave me a shock—they were so cute and it seemed like a great idea. But I couldn't stop thinking about how devilish two-and-a-half-year-old Isaac was a danger to himself. The thought of dealing with another ER visit for possible head trauma made my stomach feel queasy. That clenched feeling all over again. That carved out terror.

It was two o'clock in the afternoon and the kids were gone. The lights in the bedroom were off and Matt was in bed, talking to his mom on the phone. He had a cool cloth draped across his forehead. Joanna was begging for us to travel south for Christmas. Matt's voice was gravelly and sore from the nasogastric tubes that had been shoved in and out of his throat over the last month.

He said, "We would, Mom, but being in the car makes me feel like throwing up."

She wanted us to FedEx the gift and take the train.

"I can't, Mom," he said, pleading with her to instead make the journey north.

Joanna arrived a week before Christmas with her back trunk stuffed with two large cardboard boxes. (She wouldn't stay through the holidays; she had made other plans.) The advertising splashed across the big cardboard boxes was a picture of a pretty young mom playing with her children in a backyard the size of a small pasture. The model had her curly blonde hair pinned back and her short shorts revealed shapely legs, small knees. Her cherubic children sat in the driver's seats in the camouflaged Jeep and the pink VW Bug. Joanna gave me a loose hug. There was a big gap between our bodies. We'd shared so many traumas at the hospital, it was a shame we couldn't relate better.

I felt I had to say something about the gifts.

"I just . . . normally . . . the cars are super cute . . . maybe this year . . ." I stammered.

I finally spit it out, saying something about how I imagined the kids flipping over on the cars and the pavement crushing their little bones. Joanna laughed her nonchalant laugh and told me not to be silly. This was Christmas!

For all the exhaustion of the hospital, my mother-in-law looked as rosy-cheeked as the carefree model mom in the cardboard boxes' advertisement. I envied her cheerleader energy. Matt was sporting the black eye patch his doctors suggested wearing to exercise his bad eye. Joanna told him to please store the boxes in the garage.

She said in a giggly way, "Promise me you'll take a video Christmas morning so I can at least see the kids' faces when they open their gifts."

We made a nice dinner and watched *The Little Mermaid*. Isaac had his asthma cough and Joanna administered his inhaler. Later, upstairs scooping ice cream, Joanna pulled me aside and said, "Matt looks great, except those eyes." A tear wet her cheek. I assumed she was referencing the one stubborn swollen eye. I too feared it would stay that way forever. The one puffy eye made his face look severely lopsided and I wasn't sure how to love a man with a disfigured face. I knew it was wrong, thinking those thoughts, but I couldn't help it. That he had sight at all was remarkable and we should all be grateful.

But I knew it wasn't the puffy eye she was concerned about when she said, "I just didn't expect that stare to look so empty."

This is when it felt good to comfort someone. I told her it would get better. His flat affect would go away and later, if he needed it, we'd get him surgery or special contacts for the dilated eye. I needed to believe it; so too, did she.

"Don't worry," I said, regurgitating information I'd read on the Internet. "Recovery takes at least a year."

The next day, Matt spoke with her on the phone. He told her he wouldn't assemble the cars and that we'd return them and mail her a check. She complained: We never celebrate holidays with her! We just don't care! This went on for a half hour or so. I stood under the bedroom door frame making a silent cutting signal at my throat. It was like we were young again, or just married, and she wanted her boy back.

"I feel sick, Mom," Matt was saying, and apologized again about the cars.

I fantasized snatching the phone and reminding her how her son could barely count change, but that didn't seem right. Matt hung up, massaged his temples, and groaned. I had enchiladas in the oven and the children were watching *Tom and Jerry*. The sun was lowering fast and I could see my breath when I stepped outside with the cordless. I steadied my breathing as I dialed her number.

"I just gave Matt two Oxycodone for his headache," was how I began. "Please," I begged. "About the cars . . . I just know someone will get hurt."

At the hospital, I had complained to the mother of one of Matt's roommates, Jon, about my mother-in-law.

"They don't even get along out there," I had huffed, motioning toward the window to indicate the real world.

Jon's mother had looked at me and said, "Yes, and she's still his mother. As one yourself, surely you can understand."

I tried, but that doesn't mean it was easy. My mother had warned me this was coming; I would need to fix my boundaries—fast. But that was my mother being protective, wasn't it? Somewhere inside I knew that whatever was happening with Joanna went beyond issues about toy cars and Christmas, but I was lost in my rage and only felt a steaming red-hotness flare up inside.

When Joanna told me, "Blood is thicker than water," I snorted to show I thought she was boring.

Her son and I had said our vows and I was going to see this fucking thing through. It was awful of me when I told her to stop calling. I somewhat regretted the words as they came out of my mouth, and at the same time experienced a sense of vindication letting loose like that. I am his *wife*, I thought. This is *my* job.

"This is just plain bad behavior," I told her, and hung up.

We had begun our seven-year-long relationship with Workers' Compensation, an impenetrable bureaucratic force that understood or cared little about the complicated and subjective nature of a traumatic brain injury. I learned that Workers' Compensation is an insurance program that differs little from state to state. The basic premise for how they compensate injured workers is sometimes referred to as a "no-fault system," meaning, if a worker is injured on the job, regardless of who is to blame—worker or employer or no one—all heath care is covered, so long as it is deemed necessary by the Department of Labor. The worker is entitled to "time-loss" benefits—roughly 65 percent of earnings—while doctors recommend work accommodations while the worker receives healthcare. It is important to understand that all specialists an injured worker sees are *selected by Workers' Compensation*. If a lightened work load can't be attained, a vocational rehabilitation expert *selected by Workers' Compensation* may collaborate with the worker on a retraining plan. In Washington State, with our historic abundance of Boeing workers, Workers' Compensation became Labor & Industries (L&I), nicknamed "The Great Bargain," because using the insurance means forgoing any third-party subrogation. The bottom line is you cannot sue these guys, no matter how tragic, unfair, or long-term the injured person's condition. There will be an independent medical exam later to determine your Permanent Partial Impairment, and this will calculate your entitled Permanent Partial Disability Award.

These are not the things I worried about at the hospital. Representatives from Workers' Compensation called but I would only talk to Matt's specific claim manager, not the agents who wanted to schedule a time to visit Matt so they could create a report. One guy finally tracked me down on the phone and told me, "You shouldn't worry, ma'am. Your husband is not in jeopardy of losing his medical or time-loss benefits." I was feeling huffy, so I said, "The *patient* can't even remember what happened. How do you expect him to answer your questions?"

I didn't hear from him again until months later when they came to our house and laid out large blueprints on the kitchen table. It was like a crime scene, all those pictures with red lines and arrows. Matt seemed pleased to answer their questions, saying how he had used an old-school logger technique to rig a spar tree to cut the log from the bottom up.

You could tell the guys were thinking, "This guy is a real dipshit," but Matt drew a picture and the physics of the operation truly made sense. He explained how a veteran logger had showed him how to do it back when Matt was a helicopter copilot on a logging operation in Northern Idaho. The guys looked at me for verification and I nodded. Truth. Both men were fat and wore collared shirts with some kind of state insignia etched on their chests. The boss of the two warned me he was going to show us a picture I might not want to see. It was a photo of the bloodied tree limb, the fallen eighty-pound branch that had crashed into my husband's skull.

"The boys threw it into the chipper after we took this picture," he said.

The boys. I hadn't let myself imagine the scene until then. I had been surviving in a place where loving and praying presided over logistics or worry. Matt just sat there, unresponsive, dull.

The boss guy said something like, "What you did that day was not regulatory and you could've been killed."

I wanted to smash that guy's skull into the kitchen table then hold up his bloodied face and punch him in the mouth with spiked knuckle rings.

They left their cards and said they'd be in touch. I went to the bathroom and dry-heaved. My husband had not been wearing a helmet. *There had been no helmet.*

I was weepy in the hall, clinging to the safety of the walls for support.

Matt finally asked me, "What's wrong?" He just stared at me with those blank liquid eyes. I was mean. I called him an idiot. This was futile meanness; he didn't know what he had done. I chomped down so hard on my jaw that a piece of skin from inside my cheek ripped and I chipped a chunk of enamel from my bottom tooth.

Years later, I would request an accident report and the Department of Labor would send me the files. They had fined Matt's employer, Seattle Safe Tree Care, a mere $5,000 for neglect. I learned later in a book I read about Workers' Compensation that this is actually a large sum for a company to pay. Normally, companies are fined very little for accidents, resulting in lackluster motivation to improve upon safety practices. Seattle Safe Tree Care never designed a light work desk duty for him, and it took us four years to negotiate retraining.

At Hannah's bachelorette weekend, we made a rule that you had to wear heels to lay poolside. We stopped in dusty Vantage to shop for food and booze before heading down into Quincy Bar, an island on a river on the east side of mountains, four hours from home. We bought big slabs of carne asada from the Mexican market that we would grill for tacos and eat for leftovers all weekend long. Once we got situated in our rented condo, we went down the hill into town and bought up all the colorful hoop earrings and crazy sunglasses at this teenager store that had eight thousand pairs of teeny bikinis.

It was hard leaving Matt and the kids at home; I was glad I had such close friends to make sure I got out, though. With our new earrings and sunglasses, we laid around the pool reading foolish pulp magazines.

"If your life was a movie genre, what would it be?" Lauren said.

"Mine's totally a musical," I said, thinking about the *Hairspray* CDs I had brought as part of our swag bag gift exchange.

A vanilla-flavored illustrated sex tips book made its rounds while we flipped our bodies front to back on lounge chairs. I read a passage aloud in my best serious broadcaster voice: "A sensitive lover can elicit earth-shattering multiple, continuous, full body orgasms without penetration." My voice got all cracked and I was grateful for the sunglasses that covered my wet eyes. It had been a while since I'd had any earth-shattering sex. But no one sugarcoated the deal with platitudes—someone just handed me a fresh margarita with a penis straw.

"Whatever man wrote that," said Casey knowingly, "is a total moron." Then she did a cannonball with an impressive splash.

After dinner, we heated our curling irons and cranked '80s rock. Rumor had it there was a dive bar in town. We college girlfriends always knew where to find the dancing.

"*Ay, morena,*" a tall man whispered in my ear all night.

It was innocent when later we piled into a golf cart with a group of youngish guys, all of us sitting on each other's laps, cussing out the reckless driver when he trampled over the street's thick median. I was thinking about heads crushing against concrete: *brain injury, brain injury, brain injury.* The bride-to-be and I hopped off and walked the rest of the way. We went to the youngish guys' flop and drank light beers and played Guitar Hero.

I was so excited playing drums to Nirvana, I yelled, "Oh my God, my kids would LOVE this!"

The youngish guy singing stopped to stare. He left to pee or grab more beer and I took a hard look around us: water ski equipment, Guitar Hero, stocked bar . . . I realized they were *really that young* at the same time that I understood this cool party pad was their parents' place.

We slept in late and reminisced about how Casey had swiped a bag of their weed, laughing about how the young guys had lied, saying they were twenty-five, and how we had lied, saying we were twenty-five, too. It was fun to just be there like that, free. I could relax into another cup of coffee when I called home and learned my family had survived the night without me. Maybe, for a few special morning moments before the long drive home, life could be simple.

The early sun was heating up the pool at the private condo complex and I sat on a lounge chair with my face up toward the sun, thinking about how people sure like to golf over here, even if it's supposed to be the desert.

A lot of people felt really sorry for us. They felt so sorry for us I felt sorry for them.

There was this nice rehab specialist lady, Patsy, who was the first outpatient professional we saw after Matt was released from the hospital. The plan was to meet with her once a week in her office at the University of Washington Medical Center. Matt wasn't supposed to drive in his condition, so either I drove or he took the bus.

The schedule for outpatient rehab was inflexible and hectic. It was typical for Matt to have three different appointments in one day—all in the university district, which wasn't as far south for us as Harborview, but from our suburb required at least two buses. On days that my work schedule, Lizzie's school hours, and the appointments didn't mesh, which was often, Isaac would accompany his dad, and together they would take several city buses to the university hospital. Matt would tell me how sometimes Isaac would stand in the rain, waiting at the bus stop at the Aurora Transit Center, and scream, "I don't want to go to see Patsy!" I felt bad he was missing some preschool, and chose to hold to the idea that said this was an adventure for our small boy.

I respected Patsy because she didn't try to be cute about the situation. Isaac played around with pencils or pens or packets of sugar or whatever she had on her table. Patsy grilled Matt about his work history, and through our meetings I grilled her about grilling him. She explained how she was a vocational rehab specialist and would work in collaboration with Matt's doctors to determine next steps. I was quick to tell her that although he looked OK, he'd been severely hurt. The thought of his going to work—performing any serious task, really—was unimaginable, and if I had any strength at all those days it was proving to strangers how bad it was. I explained that even though Matt didn't have his college degree, he was a top earner, a real bright bulb.

One time Isaac was being a big turkey, jumping off the chair to land on a specific spot on her rug, and I was shushing him and he was wiggling. I got out a book I had picked up at a garage sale and began reading it to him. It was a Sesame Street book from the '70s with Big Bird on the front. The title was *I Can Do It by Myself*. Patsy didn't seem to mind. I wasn't sure yet if she would be the type to feel really sorry for us, but circumstances like these were good tests. There was a photo on her shelf of what I presumed was her family—she, her husband, and two teenage kids—on the top of a mountain posing in their North Face day-camping attire. When Patsy asked how we were doing, I said, "It's stressful, but we still manage to enjoy the children." She looked at me and blinked. I couldn't tell if she thought I was really smart or the opposite.

At first these meetings were exciting because professionals were curious about us and wanted to help us make a plan for successful re-entry into the working world. As time went on we would have to convince doctors and bureaucrats that Matt wasn't at all ready for what they wanted, and the meetings would become exhausting and irritating. I wanted to let myself be distracted with little-kid stuff, like making Play-Doh from scratch or talking to the moms at school about the reading rubric in the Bob Books. I was torn between caring for my husband and caring for my children.

My best friend from childhood was Kelly, and she didn't contact me for at least three months after the accident. But that was OK. She did other things, like leave Xanax inside tinfoil at my doorstep in an envelope with a note that said, "I love you—call me whenever you want." I had never used a regular dose before, nor would I but seldom even now. I glowed a little inside knowing an old dear friend could understand the loving space I needed. The acknowledging nod to hardship this small gesture provided made me feel seen. My other best friend, a Dutch girl I met in college named Aletta, also left me alone for a bit. She lived in the Bay Area but would call and leave messages saying things like, "It's OK, Sarah. I'm just here for you whenever, OK?"

Other friends gave up after about six months. I tried hard not to feel blame or hate toward them, but I felt sorry for myself, and was jealous of what I perceived to be their easy lives. I couldn't tell my story as I was living it without welling up or choking or making an ugly face and these things mattered to me then. But it still hurt when those friends went on with their lives without me. I imagined they were exasperated by the ambiguity of our situation. Were they scared to be close, knowing it was the kind of freak accident that could happen to anyone? Or was it me, pushing them away?

My mom sometimes grew impatient with me. "You never call me," she'd complain. It was too much, answering to everyone all the time. Now I understand that I needed them to come to me, not the other way around.

Sometimes I let myself feel as though I had a contagion. I remember once getting all dolled up for a high-school friend's engagement party. I called a high-school friend whom I felt I could trust and learned she couldn't make it. I can't remember why, but Matt couldn't go either. This was years after the accident. It was around St. Paddy's Day, and for some reason, I ratted my hair into this weird bouffant and smeared my lips with bright red lipstick. I wore a body-conscious knee-length dress I'd scored at Value Village. When I got there, the squad that I felt had ditched me was in the den taking pictures of themselves in a group. That's how they were, always in a group. I found the wine bar and downed a glass fast. I would have left early had the mother of the bride-to-be not been buzzed, bossing around her two grown sons and falling all over the fancy appetizers. It was amusing. I liked the distraction of a debacle other than mine. I clung to the bride's parents' friends who were in their sixties. When you're that age, you've seen cancer, divorce, maybe war. They asked me about Matt's recovery. I looped my arm inside one older man's elbow, feeling his loose skin against mine. He hadn't had a stroke or a seizure, but he knew he would, one day.

Something different about me was my impatience with people who I felt hadn't been down my same scalding path to hell, which of course is unfair. You didn't have to have been raped or widowed to be my friend, that's not what I'm saying. But if you hadn't figured out how to talk honestly about hard stuff, I needed to walk away. I knew before was easier, when I had more room in my heart, and I wanted to get back to that place. How long would it take? When could I even start?

Matt met with graduate student intern psychologist Barbara once a week. At first I accompanied him. It was there, in Barbara's office, where Matt said he didn't feel love. He said it plain-faced, but with concern. He knew he *should* feel something, he said. We'd been to the theatre to see the movie *Atonement* and he told her how my sniffling at the end confused him, how everyone's wet eyes didn't make sense.

"It's like I'm alone and thirsty in the desert," he'd told her. "There is a glass of water within my reach. I can see it and I want it but I can't figure out how to get it."

I could tell Barbara thought he was brilliant. It seemed the thing to do, according to Barbara, was to treat recovery as a scientist would, with a sense of simple curiosity. Could we give that a try? And practice smiling in the mirror. Every day make faces at yourself. Treat this as a fun way to get to know yourself again, and don't worry too much.

Matt needed a second surgery to repair his temporal wasting. Atrophied muscles had caused his skin to sink into his left temple. The way I understood it, the skin would continue to sink into his face and his face would further droop and take on the appearance of lopsidedness. Dr. Mann was the surgeon who had performed Matt's inpatient surgeries, and he would do this one, too. So long as we had Workers' Compensation, we might as well have it done.

Dr. Mann would remove fat from Matt's thigh and inject it into the sunken area. Joanna accompanied Matt for the second surgery. I told myself I had PTSD and couldn't go back to the trauma center. Afterward Joanna reported how they took fat from Matt's abdomen since there was none in his thighs. I knew there would be jokes later, and indeed when I shared the new absurd update my funny mom friends said things like, "Oh, you should have told me . . . I would have volunteered to have my thigh lard removed."

I investigated underneath his soiled bandages. The black-and-blue tracks across his lower belly looked like a loaded train had gunned him down and it reminded me of the nip-and-tuck TV shows that make you swear you'll never, no matter what, go under the knife. The area on his temple was a little lumpy, but Joanna said Dr. Mann had explained that it would smooth out. The added flesh made him appear more like his old self.

"You look great, babe," I said, feeling buoyed and grateful.

Life was manageable as a checklist, and since now his face was put back together, all we had to do was figure how to fix that dilated pupil. Next, find a good dentist. Then, strategize a solid back-to-work plan.

I wanted to take Matt's claim manager out to lunch. It was starting to look like we would be taking the long route toward recovery, so I figured we could be friends.

"I'll come down to you," I said, meaning I'd drive to the state capitol, where the Department of Labor offices were.

"That's really not necessary," she said.

Joy was her name. Joy's job was to approve Matt's doctor's visits. She paid hospital bills and cut his time-loss checks every two weeks. When he was first hurt and the nurses and my dad helped me file the claim, Joy had called the hospital and asked to talk to me directly.

"I'm so sorry to hear about all of this," she had said.

I could tell she meant it. Her voice was deep and gravelly with a slight twang, like she was midwestern. It made me think of my aunt Kathleen, who was funny and strong. Six months later, when Matt began managing his health care, he mused over her just like I did. "I bet she's Native," he said. "Why?" I asked. "She just sounds like it, and with a name like Naveaga . . . there's that Quinault Nation on the coast and sometimes they come down to Olympia for work. Or the Nisqually—that could be it." I never understood how he knew these things. "I bet she's big and has kids and is the boss of her department," said Matt.

"Really?" I asked. "Why?"

"I don't know," he said. "Just because."

Once I asked Joy to write a threatening-sounding letter to the private physicians who had billed us for Matt's emergency room visit when he had had his seizure. Labor & Industries hadn't paid it yet, and the physicians group had sent us to collections. We couldn't pay it and our credit score was getting dinged.

"Sure, I'll do it," she said. "No problem."

"Can I ask you a question?" I said.

"Sure," Joy said.

"How many clients do you have?" I asked.

"I manage about three hundred claims," she said.

I cleared my throat. "Hey, do people ever, you know, get lawyers for this sort of thing?"

"Here in Washington State, Labor & Industries doesn't support third-party subrogation. But there's always the Board of Appeals," she said.

I told her those were big words for me.

"I can't really give you advice," she said, "but it's all online."

I was OK with that; I could always do research later.

"One more thing," I said.

"Sure," she said.

I was feeling pretty glad Joy was talking to me for so long on the phone.

I asked her, "Are all your clients' cases as serious as Matt's?" Her keyboard went click-click.

"Sure," she said. "There are really serious accidents all the time."

Lizzie wears a prim lace sundress. Her hair is in French braids. Isaac is wearing a polo shirt. He is using sticks for guns. Matt is a Best Man and makes a toast in the dark. It's a slurred speech about the bride being Zach's one and only. I hide in the shadows. The next day I organize our bags. I ask Matt to coordinate with another family to get the booster seats they'd borrowed. At first he lies on the futon with a wet cloth over his head, and then he disappears. I find him an hour later, wandering around, trying to remember what it was he was supposed to do.

A friend says, "Is that normal since the accident?"

I say, "Yeah, when he drinks."

"That's gotta be hard," she says.

I want to cry. I shove our clothes in our suitcase. It's hard because we're in a little cabin by a raging river and I can't let the kids out of my sight. In the car, I watch the mirages on the hot pavement. I stare ahead and my knuckles get white gripping the wheel. I want the distraction of the radio, but any sounds hurt his head, so we listen to the whirring hum of the air conditioner. He takes four Excedrin every two hours and drapes a wet cloth around his neck. His eyes stay shut until we arrive at his mom's house, three hours later.

◆ ◆ ◆

(a letter)

Hey.

Hey, remember the office out back at the first house? I set it up with a treadmill and attached that little TV to the wall. You found a newt in the backyard and put it on Lizzie's shoulder. We brought Isaac home to that house. I quit my teaching job and hand-washed all the bottles. I painted the trim a peanut butter color. You built a brick patio, a fence, a deck, two raised garden beds, and a garden shed. You used white spray paint to etch leaf imprints on the red front door. When we moved, the sand box my dad built would come with us, same with the rhubarb plant. Remember the crazy paint job in Isaac's room? You mastered it in one long weekend—

all those bright colors. It looked like a carousel or a stick of colorful sugar gum. Outside with the moving truck we took one last look at the little yellow house. You hardly did this kind of thing, but you did for me then. You said, "Don't cry. We'll do it to the next one, too. Just the same."

What about the handrail you shaved down from a branch? You saved a piece of cedar from work, knowing it was the perfect size for the set of stairs heading to the foyer in the new house. When we bought the new place, we made a lot of plans, but then we moved in and realized the bigger the house, the more money it takes to fix stuff. After we ripped up carpets and finished the wood floors and painted, we were spent. Still, you had all the neighbor kids out front on the lawn with drawknives to peel away the bark. You paid them fresh dollar bills to use fine grit sandpaper to smooth it down. Every person who touches that handrail in the foyer comments on its smoothness. It's like butter, or a baby's bottom, or silk, they say. One neighbor tried to commission you to make her one, remember? But it's like my dad and his side projects, like the wooden crib he built for Lizzie when she was born. It looked like something out of a craftsman furniture catalog, right? Someone would buy that for like three hundred dollars, I told my dad, but he sort of snorted and said, yeah, but it took me three months to make.

◆ ◆ ◆

10/06/2008
8:00 AM

Last night was one of the scariest nights of my life. Matt had a seizure, only I thought he was dying. I woke up to his arms swinging into me and I thought shit, shit, shit, this is it. I tore through the house all breathless and naked and of course could not find the phone. I heard Isaac rustling in his upper bunk across the hall and there was a loud THUD as Matt's head banged the back of our stupid modern bed. I put a pillow beneath his head and yelled to Isaac from my room I was going to the neighbors' and would be right back. I caught Mari in her nightgown and she stood frozen under the doorframe holding her dog by its collar. My throat was all scratchy and I jumped up and down and asked her to call 911 and to do it NOW and she totally did, ran like a banshee and got her husband Tim who was really good and sweet about the whole thing. Matt must have been convulsing for five minutes because when we got back to our bedroom his face was blue and his body was limp. There was a pool of saliva on his cheek and his eyes were rolled back into his skull and his flaccid penis was exposed and I felt so awful, I covered him up with the sheets and checked on Lizzie, who was sleeping like a rock. I heard Tim say look Mari, he's breathing, and so I took Isaac to the bathroom, sat him on the stool by the heater, and kissed his wet chubby cheeks. Tim cooed to Matt and everyone was relieved when the medics arrived and the lead EMT checked Matt's pulse and said he'd probably had a grand mal seizure, which are scary to see, but are easily treated. (Note to self: Maybe when Matt gets better he can be a medic. They are hot and heroic.) Dude wanted to know if it was his first seizure and I really didn't understand the relevance but I nodded, telling my heart to slow down. Like always, and because they are kind (not evil as I would prefer them), the medical team wanted to know why, what, when, who, so I told them about the head injury a year before and they all nodded because apparently, it's common after a TBI. Apparently. Matt always begins sentences with that word now and I hate it: apparently this, apparently that. Because he's not sure of anything for certain. So anyways the team assisted Matt walking down the steps and into the ambulance and all the lights in the cul-de-sac came alive and dogs began to bark. On the way back from the hospital a neighbor stopped in her minivan to find out what had happened. She talked to me with the window rolled down halfway. She told me it was remarkable what I've done, and how most couples don't make it through lesser tragedies. Take it from me, she said. I ought to know. I've been on disability for years now. It's no cakewalk. She talked as though we had already passed through this tragedy, when really we're knee-deep in it, especially now that this has happened. Fuck! The only comforting thing is what Noelle said, and she's seen a bunch of shit, AND she's a nurse. She said maybe his mind needed a reset button pushed and this did the trick. I will use that line when I hold back these thick throaty pills of tears explaining the development of a seizure disorder. I just fucking hate all those disappointed faces. He's supposed to be getting better. I'll say the brain is like a computer and his got a reboot.

11/05/2008
9:00 PM

Today Matt and I dressed up like Maya and Miguel and gave out PBS stickers and pencils to all the kids at Evergreen Elementary. Lizzie's teacher took a Polaroid I am looking at right now while I drink my tea. Lizzie is wearing what I call her Punky Brewster outfit and OMG Isaac looks so cute in jeans and a T-shirt underneath a black-and-white-checked sweater vest. Lizzie has this proud look on her face, like check out my parents, they're so cool. Isaac is looking sidelong at us in our enormous cartoon bobbleheads, totally weirded out by the whole situation. I love being in her classroom. The smells of the dry-erase boards, the little rubbery shavings of old-fashioned pink erasers. And her teachers are so cool. I was there the morning of Obama's win. I took a seat in a little kid's chair with Lizzie on my lap and cried a little. The whole election season has been exciting, but that also means Christmas is coming, which means more spending what we don't have. Workers' Comp is working out OK, but the loss of income is catching up with us. "Like squeezing water from a rock," Matt likes to say. I guess it always works out, somehow. The whole country is up in arms about the Great Recession, which, I have to say, doesn't really affect us. From what I understand, people with jobs are losing them, and people with high mortgages are going "under." I'm hearing on the news people with two or three houses are claiming bankruptcy. I'm not trying to be a grouch, but that seems kind of sneaky, or just plain wrong. On a really bad day, I want to walk around the neighborhood screaming, "Who cares about your bills! This man here was nearly dead twice!" Ugh. I want to be one of those chicks who's always like, "It's all good," or "No worries," but I can't because that's such bullshit, a total cop-out. I think there are degrees of suffering, and ours is pretty up there. I am regularly annoyed at family dinner when my parents complain about their stocks plummeting. And then I just feel bad, like I'm an ungrateful, useless person. That's probably why I'm irritable; I'm just jealous of their problems.

04/02/2009
6:00 AM

I'm reading the RCWs online on the Labor & Industries website right now and feeling like I want to puke. The Department of Labor's main objective is to get injured workers working, preferably with the same company at time of injury, and a vocational counselor's job is to put together a plan for gainful employment. Blah, blah, blah. The way they categorize everyone like they're all the same just grosses me out. We're all just like Kafka's beetle, no better than roaches scurrying around trying to get a nibble from whatever we can find on the cold hard ground. So depressing! Who can even understand any of this stuff?

RCW 51.08.180 "Worker"—Exceptions.

"Worker" means every person in this state who is engaged in the employment of an employer under this title, whether by way of manual labor or otherwise in the course of his or her employment; also every person in this state who is engaged in the employment of or who is working under an independent contract, the essence of which is his or her personal labor for an employer under this title, whether by way of manual labor or otherwise, in the course of his or her employment, or as an exception to the definition of worker, a person is not a worker if he or she meets the tests set forth in subsections (1) through (6) of RCW 51.08.195 or the separate tests set forth in RCW 51.08.181 for work performed that requires registration under chapter 18.27 RCW or licensing under chapter 19.28 RCW: PROVIDED, That a person is not a worker for the purpose of this title, with respect to his or her activities attendant to operating a truck which he or she owns, and which is leased to a common or contract carrier.

05/15/2009
7:00 AM

I feel like I only write in this when bad stuff happens, so this time I'll report on something cute. There was a talent show at school last night and Lizzie and her best friend Selah performed on stage with their dads. I sat with Joanna and Selah's mom, Julia, in the stands with my video recorder. The girls dressed like twins with brown corduroy pants, black turtlenecks, and bright red bandanas. OMG it was SO adorable the way they prepared a little performance, snapping their fingers and swinging their hips to a tune the guys wrote over beers and hot wings. David played guitar and Matt played harmonica and sang, which when he does I'm always so surprised how good he is! Here's the funny part: Matt was totally high on Oxy for the show. He removed his head bandage and wore a ball cap so no one could see the stitched-over incision on the side of his forehead from the terrific liposuction he just had. Oxycodone for the pain plus a Valium and the way he looked out at the audience I could tell that to him, we were a sea of imaginary fans. He was all outgoing and stuff, making introductions and calling everyone beautiful like five different times. I was worried, but I told myself if Julia, who is a seriously worried Jewish mother, was cool with it, I could be, too. (The show must go on, right?) The song, we learned as we listened, was about the daily chore of selecting a choice from the school lunch menu, namely, a chicken burger. Isaac totally boogied in the front row and Joanna and I were getting along great. The chorus was easy and everyone followed along. Julia was all, See? Aren't you glad he came out? Later that night, Lizzie was sitting in the kitchen trying to do her math problems. She does this thing where she gazes at her reflection in the sliding glass door window. Matt told her to focus on her math problems, but we laughed, knowing her ego is healthy. These are the moments I feel regular. It was a good day!

05/30/2009
1:00 AM

Last week was super-duper crazy. I went to Portland for a workshop training where they paid me like $200 to facilitate a PBS curriculum about childhood obesity for a group of at-home childcare providers sponsored by SEIU Local 925. I got there the night before to hang out with Casey and Lauren and we went shopping at Palace Place for cheap tank tops since it was freakishly hot. Then we ate Mexican and got wasted sitting on the patio after getting sunburned, just walking around town in our new tank tops. We ordered pitchers of margaritas and those two were so nice to me, listening and asking good questions about how everything's been. Afterward we walked down the street to some reggae bar and smoked cigarettes and joints and really raged hard, hard enough that I wanted to PUKE the next day in that teeny conference room with too much body heat and no air conditioning in a hundred-plus degrees. Later I felt so gross I pulled over on the side of the road on my way home and slept for like an hour. When I got home, Matt had a surprise: he bought us tickets to Matisyahu! Even though his emotional disconnection is unsettling, he has these moments of total sincerity. We had the kids at my parents' house overnight and ate dinner with them first and my mom admired my outfit and my dad hadn't heard of Matisyahu. We were sort of surprised that we were the oldest ones at the theater, and I did feel kinda old, since it was so loud and we were using ear plugs. I'm playing the new CD in the car every day, and there's this cool song with machine-gun sounding noises Isaac loves. I can feel the creases in my forehead doubling twofold with all this fast-moving stuff in life, some is fun and I can't really complain, but I also keep imagining just resting somewhere for a week, somewhere quiet.

◆ ◆ ◆

We all learned about Matt's residual challenges together, but if the learning was a race, I was in the lead. As a leader, I became impatient when those trailing behind were too slow to keep up.

Like the time my dad asked Matt to climb the mast of his sailboat to screw tight an important bolt. I watched the kids as they bent over the dock, touching purple anemones. I fingered the varnished topcoat on the boat's wooden deck. Matt was the only one who could fit into the climbing harness. I volunteered to do it and all three men laughed. The men rigged ropes and hoisted him up the mast.

I yelled, "Are you OK up there?" and he looked down, giving a two-handed thumbs-up and a wide grin.

Later, he told me the truth—that he had been scared. It was always reassuring to me when Matt expressed sincere concerns. He told me how the mast was so tall it swayed harder than the top of any tree. It made me think of the time my brother hired Matt to remove the old-growth fir tree in the lot he and Malia bought next door, how she had called Matt a total stud, not like she lusted over him, but with real respect.

But this time was different: didn't they remember the hospital? Was I really the only one that understood the severity of his long-term injuries? What's with the danger and risk? I turned my back from the scene to walk Lizzie and Isaac to the shore. We watched a pelican on a rock. I could only control so much, and keeping the kids entertained made me feel safe.

We used to go to Matt's grandparents' cabin in Diamond Peak with the kids and family friends. They called it the Lodge. It was always a long stressful drive with kids, but once you settled into the A-frame by the river, it was easy to find a way to relax.

I noticed something that looked like white glue smeared down the full-length mirror in the living room. I asked Matt if it was bat guano, and he shrugged. I showed him a carcass the size of my palm I'd found in the bathroom.

"Yes, in summer they like to eat the bugs."

"But guano . . . isn't that poisonous?"

I wanted to know what he planned to do about the bats. He was always a boss like that, and fixing stuff was no problem. Lizzie stopped mid-spoonful and pointed to a small flying object.

"Look, there's a bird," she said.

We were used to critters in the Lodge. Matt always cleared mouse droppings and set traps. We let the kids think it was a bird. Why not? That night, something whistled through my hair as I was trying to sleep.

"Hey," I whispered to Matt. "Is there a bat flying around?"

He laughed at me and turned over to sleep. The next morning, our friend David saw it, too. We knew it was a bat but we didn't say anything because we knew David's wife Julia would freak out. It flew over the rafters in the kitchen while the kids ate their cereal and Matt chopped wood on the porch.

"Look!" Lizzie pointed.

The bat zigzagged through the air in slow motion. I looked at David. David looked at Matt, who had just entered the front door with a bundle of kindling in his arms. Julia screamed, "Matt, do something!"

By the time Matt got the paper bag from the kitchen, the bat had flown into the bathroom.

"What are you going to do?" I asked him. I pictured the bat shitting all over the wall.

"Wait here," he told us.

We heard a loud thump and some shrieking. I pictured it using its bat wings to slap Matt around. A door slammed. A wall shook. This noise parade went on for three minutes. Then it was silent.

"Don't kill it, Daddy!" yelled Lizzie.

Matt came out and wiped his sweaty brow, held up a bag and said, "Got him."

Matt usually passed out after a long day in the sun, but that night he didn't. It was hard to tell what caused brain drain and what did not. Earlier we'd been in town drinking cucumber martinis and it was a hundred degrees. Before that we'd been underground inside primordial lava tunnels. Julia took me aside and said, "I just can't believe he has a brain injury. It doesn't seem like anything's wrong."

That trip we took a picture of Matt posing with his Grandpa Jimmy's atlatl, an Aztec tool for spear throwing. Being at the Lodge I romanticized love a lot, probably because we'd spent good times there when we were younger, before the accident, before kids. I hoped Matt would continue to get better, and I hoped for myself I could be patient.

Top Market was the name of the grocery store where I shopped. You could fill up your large cart to last past a week for way under two hundred dollars. The produce was fresh, like an outdoor farmer's market; I liked the bakery and hot food bar. It was open twenty-four hours, so sometimes I shopped after the kids were in bed. I would plug in my earbuds and cruise the aisles looking for the perfect six-ounce jar of black sliced olives. If it was daytime and Lizzie went with me, I'd remind her how I used to push her and Isaac in the red racecar shopping cart when they were littler. The seat belts were always lined with a layer of crumbs, I told her, just like the bottom of my car floor. I'd remind her how I would bribe her and Isaac with little Dum Dum suckers so they might be good and still.

I liked putting away eggs and sour cream and tortillas and ice cream and chicken breasts and bagged salads and juice boxes and cookies. It made me feel useful, like I was contributing to growth and well-being. I remember once when Lizzie was with me and we were shopping for a baby shower I was going to host. I was thinking of making this recipe I saw online where you stuff prosciutto and minced pears inside a mini-muffin tin and bake it for ten minutes. We headed to the area with the fancy cheeses and meats and crackers. A handful of fresh, organic purple grapes would be pretty draped with cheese and crackers over my porcelain white raised cake stand. She pointed sheepishly at the stuffed animals by the flower shop.

I said, smiling, "For the baby, or for you?"

At the checkout, the numbers rose with my nerves. I put in the code for my Top Market discount card. My debit card didn't go through and the checker lady looked bored. She announced something on the speaker and told me I could leave the cart there, if I wanted to. I had a little cash, so I paid for the eggs, milk, bread and toilet paper. It was painful sending Lizzie back to the flower shop area with the stuffed doggie. I hadn't grown up poor, so setting modest budgets and sticking with them was hard. Matt sat on the couch in front of the TV back home. I told him what had happened.

Without looking up he said, "Because of me, we're poor. It's all my fault."

We got in this rhythm of meeting once a week during my lunch break with a life coach named Lydia. I was having the obvious troubles and would bemoan the pressures over work, Matt's progress, house projects, children. Lydia noted my tiredness and asked me to show her what I thought the word *resignation* looked like. I sort of hunched my shoulders and slumped into the couch. Thinking about the four-syllable word reminded me how much I used to love a good spelling bee. In grade school, back in the '80s, I used to place among the top in my class, moving into the all-school contest. I remember feeling ashamed on stage, in front of the school, when I lost to the word "pitcher" because I thought the judge said "picture." I spent the rest of the week hating myself for not having asked the judge to use it in a sentence.

When Lydia asked Matt what the word *resignation* looked like to him, he was asleep on the couch. She asked me to continue on with just her in private sessions, and I did, sneaking away when I could from my desk job at the TV station. She thought I was a true leader and wanted me to consider her Life Coach Training Program, a thing that felt lofty and presumptuous to me. Perhaps it was clear to her that though I exhibited leadership, I was lost and needed direction. I remember how amongst the women in her Life Coach Training Introductory Session, she introduced me as someone who had been wounded, but was recovering. I reddened in front of my small audience. I knew she meant well, but I still did not want to be seen that way. The definition of "resign" from Merriam-Webster's dictionary is this:

Full Definition of *RESIGN*
transitive verb

    1: relegate, consign; *especially*: to give (oneself) over without resistance

    2: to give up deliberately; *especially*: to renounce (as a right or position) by a formal act
intransitive verb

    1: to give up one's office or position: quit

    2: to accept something as inevitable: submit

Judge, can you use that word in a sentence?

"She resigned her position as caregiver when the patient never recovered."

◆ ◆ ◆

UNDATED

I CANNOT stop thinking about that hospital. I keep seeing
Matt's comatose body enter into a CAT scan machine. How
the technician was a deadhead-looking man in his fifties whose
long, dark, curly hair was tucked inside a red bandana. How his
bushy eyebrows were wild, like he'd stuck his finger in an electrical socket. How he asked me if I was the Wife. How it was 2
a.m. and I had been there, alone, with Deadhead and the other
technician, a lady with a blonde bob and Mickey Mouse Scrubs.
How they sat drinking black coffee. My stomach remembers
the tight feeling I'd get, as though clenching my muscles hard
would prevent any worse news. I remember how Mickey Mouse
Scrubs lady used the X-ray scanner's zoom feature to narrow in
on Matt's fractures. How the bones were smaller than I expected and how the breaks looked clean. How Matt's skull reminded me of a tectonic plate. How the screen showed a foggy nebula
in the right frontal lobe of his brain. How any kind of smallish
bones remind me of the chicken bones my mother used to save
and dry by the windowsill for my brother and me to wish upon,
then tug. How Deadhead said to me, "Your husband might be
in here a while." How people kept telling me how we were in
the right place for trauma, how survivors of burns and head injuries are flown from all over the Northwest for superior medical treatment from top-dog surgeons—oh how I wish I could
stop remembering! How we are "lucky," how I used to nod like
I was so grateful. How Mickey Mouse Scrubs spoke to Deadhead as though I was not in the room. How she had said, "I'm
guessing Otolaryngology then inpatient rehab." How Mickey

Mouse Scrubs asked Matt's age, and how I told her he's turning thirty-three next week and how she nodded as if to say, good, good, youth is on his side. How Deadhead guy's grin was super lopsided. How Mickey Mouse Scrubs changed the radio to something more electronic and moody. How he cringed at her choice and took a swill of his coffee. How he asked me if we had kids and how my tongue had completely outgrown my mouth, how if I opened my lips my tongue would have rolled out on to the floor in a snaky unraveling, like the kids' pink bubble gum tape. How I held up two fingers. How Deadhead looked me up and down. How he said, "It's not going to be easy, but you seem solid." How I asked where I could please find one of those cups of coffee. (And how I wanted to ask, Will that cloudy nebula in his frontal lobe ever clear?) How he got all bossy, and said, "A little advice, sweetheart? Not too much caffeine. Make rest a priority else you'll burn out. Trust me, I see it all the time. You got people in town, or are you staying at the First Hill Apartments?" How I told him I was lucky—I have my parents who live in Magnolia. How a low whir signaled the CAT scan was done, how it spit Matt out looking as lifeless as he did going in. How Matt's wrists and ankles were secured inside restraints and a thick white karate-style belt bound his chest. How his eyes were glued shut with a crusty egg-yolk-drizzle seal. How Deadhead guy made a call and two tall orderlies showed up in ten seconds. How I feared the real agenda was to take Matt to an ancient tomb inside a pyramid where plans for his mummification were underway. How I followed the orderlies out with Matt's limp body. How Deadhead said, "Lady, I hope to never see you here again." How I inhaled the hand sanitizer smell from my palm as we began our journey upstairs to floor five and how I thought about what Deadhead had said. You seem solid.

What bullshit. How my legs felt about as solid as the Pyrex dish of raspberry Jell-O Lizzie and I had made the week before for the Bear Scare party at her school. How Matt smelled like metal and excrement but the medical coma under which he slept seemed peaceful and I was jealous. How Matt shifted his torso a bit, more of an unconscious maneuver than a movement of discomfort, for he was in a dreamland, or non-dreamland, but either way gone. How the orderlies talked amongst each other using their native language and tightened the chest restraint as we entered the elevator. How that hospital was such a ward, with nasty stuff littering the floor. How I was disgusted seeing an inside-out plastic blue glove, or a wadded-up piece of Kleenex, or a cigarette butt. How I didn't have time for a meager cup of hospital coffee. How I could not let my husband out of sight.

◆ ◆ ◆

I wanted a third child, despite overwhelming stressors. I thought it might make things better. I remember having lunch with a lovely mom friend who was always such a good listener. We sat outside in the winter sun sipping lattes with our youngest children—we both had boys in preschool. She was pregnant with her fourth. Her church had put us on their prayer list and her mom group had given us a gift card to the grocery store. I kissed Isaac's chubby cheeks.

"You should have a baby," she said. "When this is over, it will be like a new beginning."

I thought of it the same way. I had so much to hope for. Then I thought about the sense of smell, how it ignites emotions, memory, and how Matt hadn't recovered his yet, how if we had a baby he wouldn't be able to smell its delicious baby head.

Once, I smelled rotten milk downstairs and scavenged around, searching for empty bottles beneath the couch. I couldn't find any and the smell got worse. The children and I left so Matt could MacGyver the situation. We returned from errands to find Matt's head inside torn-up drywall, his leather tool belt around his hips, every pocket filled with a different harsh chemical product.

"It's rats," he said, feeling triumphant.

He had scoured the space in the ceiling where the two rats had died. He planted traps with pieces of peanut butter candy bars to kill the rest.

"And you didn't smell anything the whole time?"

He shook his head. No, he still couldn't smell a thing.

Years later, when Matt and I separated and met for the kid exchange in Portland, he told us this story over breakfast:

He'd been painting the hangar floor at work using a special ventilator he'd rented for the job. That night, at a party, he drank two beers and felt awful. He got his keys out to drive himself home, but by the time he sat down in the driver's seat he must have passed out, because, as he said, "When I woke up it was morning."

I don't know how the kids feel when this stuff comes up. I feel myself want to mother him, but I stop, because he does not need that from me. I think I asked him if he told his work what had happened, but I can't remember what he said. If he said yes, it probably didn't make me feel better.

◆ ◆ ◆

06/20/2012
10:00 PM

We saved a thousand bucks from our tax return and took a family trip to Vancouver, BC. I planned it all out. We bought train tickets and traveled with our bikes and backpacks. Matt attached bells on each of our bikes so we were all, "beep beep, on your left!" We stayed at an older, small boutique hotel which felt like one of those old-fashioned spots where writers might pay to stay by the night. The residential street was tree-lined and there was an Italian restaurant in a courtyard below. The lobby had black and white photographs of historic Vancouver sites and the wooden hallways creaked. Rooms weren't air-conditioned, the bathroom was tiny, and the windows were not safely secured. It was hot and stuffy but the kids loved it. We biked the eight-mile path along View Park Drive around the bay. We passed Lions Gate Bridge and about a billion little parks. We stopped and saw beluga whales at the aquarium, swam in the saltwater pool adjacent to the sea, and showered beneath man-made caverns at the outdoor water park beside some significant historical arch. Lizzie's favorite thing was Turtle Lake, where we watched a family of water turtles sunbathe and beavers floating and building, and where blue herons were diving for crayfish. One morning we ate warm chocolate brioche at a café and walked to the installation of Chinese artist Yue Minjun's fourteen bronze statues of a shirtless guy in different poses laughing hysterically. For dinner, we ate fresh sushi and later that night had gelato on Locust Street. We were true tourists, a normal family! Everywhere we went Matt ordered me Bloody Marys! I have this great picture of the four of us standing atop a monument with the words printed in caps: PRAYER PEAK. The last night of our trip was the best—we left the kids in the room alone to watch the summer Olympics and had a date night in the romantic Italian restaurant at the street level. I wore a white seersucker knee-length skirt and a lavender cotton blouse. He wore his red collared shirt and cargo shorts. Matt ordered us a bottle of Chianti and butternut squash ravioli and a green salad to share. Matt opened up that night, I mean really shared. Everything he said started with "I remember," or "I feel." Usually he acts like he'd rather forget it all, which I can understand, even though it's hard for me. My mom, the therapist, always says he if he really thinks about what happened to his body he might struggle getting out of bed. But that night he talked about Enrique, the smallish Mexican guy on the tree crew, who at the scene of the accident couldn't really understand what Matt had been saying. Matt said, "I mean, I'm not pointing fingers because an accident is an accident, but if Enrique hadn't let go of the brakes, the truck would have stayed put and the spar tree would have stuck." I asked him if he remembered having dinner at Azteca the night before, or the windstorm the week before, and he couldn't. He remembered getting wheeled along by an orderly in the hospital and left alone for hours before someone got him. He did not remember his puffy hands but for the first time when I explained how the CDC came in for a spinal tap he acted curious. He asked me to describe how his voice sounded when he woke and I tried my best to imitate the high-pitched nasal squeak he made after surgery. He asked me to explain about the surgery and the waiting and I did. He wanted to know about Teddy's phone call and everyone's reaction to the ordeal and I told him. Then he said, "That must have been really hard for you."

UNDATED

When we were at the hospital, I used to imagine making plans for hosting a big party to celebrate Matt's recovery. I had this fantasy of how in a year we'd rent a great big facility with a DJ and a disco ball and a caterer and all our friends, all the lovely people who had prayed and visited and donated time and money, would come and we could thank them. It's looking more and more like that's not going to happen. People have pretty much moved on and I don't blame them. Matt has everyone fooled that he's OK, and I don't blame him for that, either. I can't imagine what it would be like to basically lose memories or have severe headaches or forget how to feel. But he's not OK, or he is, but he's not the man I married. It's not ever going to be the way it was. I wish I could go back a few years to when he was just out of the hospital and there was more hope. Matt was worrying about silly shit then, like the time he put up this big fuss about how the surgeons had removed the mole that was behind his ear. His brother and Joanna were there—I remember it so clearly, because it was as if the three of us were in on a joke. Matt was fingering behind his ear, saying, "They should have asked me first," about the mole! He didn't realize they were likely doing him a favor, since the mole was large and in the way of an incision they needed to make to save his life. His brother made a joke, saying, "Yeah, because you really needed that, bro," and Matt didn't get it. Joanna is such an airhead she thought it was hilarious, and his reaction was kinda funny at the time, but now I see how his thinking hasn't changed that much. He couldn't see then how a cut-out mole wasn't that big of a deal compared to what happened to his body, but then again, it's his body, his mole. I can understand his concern, actually, about being respected by doctors, but what's not funny at all, and what continues to be a problem, is this focus on really small stuff. Rather than worrying about work, he worries about which color of ski jacket to buy himself. I still want to go back to when it was fresh though, when I thought it would be a year and everything would be fine, and we'd be these conquerors of the biggest battle of our lives. Back when it was amusing how he took off in the Explorer that night on New Year's Eve when it snowed. It was only six months or so after his seizure and he wasn't supposed to drive. He was on this awful medication because we hadn't figured out the Lamictal yet. But he had to make those fresh tracks in the road. It was amusing because that's the part about him I love. His sense of adventure, his lust for life—corny thing to say but 100 percent true. I would never in a million years have gotten upset with him for rallying in a four-wheel drive vehicle in the snow, and even then, I thought it was kind of cute when Hannah called to tell me Matt had arrived at their house for the party they had canceled. It was amusing then, but now I'm just fucking tired and really wish I could just bury my head in the sand until . . . I don't know when.

◆ ◆ ◆

The movie *The Sessions* is based on the life of Mark O'Brien, the late American poet and advocate for people with disabilities. My friend Hannah and I went to see it. We met beforehand to grab noodles at a pho spot on Aurora Avenue. Hannah was pregnant and I was in graduate school studying scripts because I thought I wanted to write a movie. My adviser had recommended I see the film because it was based on an essay O'Brien wrote called "On Seeing a Sex Surrogate" that appeared in *The Sun Magazine* in 1990. In it, he describes how he wished to lose his virginity, and through the help of his priest and therapist, contacted a professional sex surrogate to get the job done. O'Brien contracted polio in 1955 and spent the rest of his life paralyzed and trapped inside an iron lung.

He writes:

"I asked Cheryl whether she thought I deserved to be loved sexually. She said she was sure of it. I nearly cried. She didn't hate me. She didn't consider me repulsive. . . . Back home, Dixie put me into the iron lung and set up my computer so that I could write. Pounding the keys with my mouth stick, I wrote in my journal as quickly as I could about my experience, then switched off the computer and tried to nap. But I couldn't. I was too happy. For the first time, I felt glad to be a man." He wrote all that in 1986. Then, in 1990, he backpedaled, suggesting he had been too optimistic about the experience with Cheryl: "My desire to love and be loved sexually is equaled by my isolation and my fear of breaking out of it. The fear is twofold. I fear getting nothing but rejections. But I also fear being accepted and loved. For if this latter happens, I will curse myself for all the time and life that I have wasted."

The narrative is voice-over with lots of bits of O'Brien's lovely poetry. But we also get a slice of Cheryl's life. I caught myself wondering what it was that motivated Cheryl to become a sex surrogate for people with disabilities. How did her husband feel about that—what about her teenage son? Helen Hunt played Cheryl, and there was this scene where she stood entirely nude in full daylight. She looked great!

When we left the theatre, I felt a little bad I had chosen this film to take a pregnant woman to see, since it was so heavy. As we got in the car to head home, I told Hannah something stupid, like, "It's a good thing we have a vaccine for polio now." I spent all afternoon with a warm sensation in my belly. I felt grateful knowing we are all in our own way a little differently-abled.

Sometimes I would sneak one of Matt's leftover Oxycodones. Never having been one for painkillers, he insisted he leave the hospital with as few as possible. But I wanted something that could relieve the pressure, or fill the emptiness, though they never worked to do either. I'd eat a corner of one and drive around the neighborhood listening to Frank Ocean. I'd park by condos with beach views and imagine how nice it would be sell the troublesome fixer house and just live there by the sea in peace. I'd consider the happy-seeming couples at the parties we'd go to and wonder what it was about me that wanted that so bad. It wasn't the vacations or the clothes or the jobs, but the *connection* it seemed like they enjoyed with each other. I was envious of what I imagined were their stressors, like which summer camps to send their kids too, or how to find a quality math tutor. I knew that may have been petty, but I couldn't help it. I wanted a strong connection. I wanted security.

I heard my mom's voice in my head, saying something she told me when I asked her back in the day how you knew it was the right person or time to get married. She had told me something like, "You can be different from each other, but you must share the same values and dream about the same things."

It was wise advice—in Matt I had met an equal. But things had changed. This was the beginning of my guilt: knowing I would be the one to break up our family. Sitting in the dark inside the parked, running car I'd think about what I was learning in graduate school—the importance of nouns and specificity and the hierarchy of important events. One adviser had taught me about learning your characters' deal—the stuff that makes one tick, and for an exercise in group we did a grown-up Mad Libs game where we filled in the rest of a sentence that began with, "He was the kind of guy/girl who (fill in the blank)." So, when I was driving home high I came up with these:

- He is the kind of guy who makes homemade Valentine's cards with doilies.
- He is the kind of guy who finds the best deal for electric ski boot warmers.
- He is the kind of guy who can identify names of aircraft engines.
- He is the kind of guy who calls his mother by her first name.

Three or so years after the accident, Matt was assigned Bobbi, a vocational counselor whose office was down the street. She was a cool brunette who looked like she could be on TV, like a Tina Fey or someone else attractive in a wholesome way like that.

"Matt," she said, "I can see you are a hardworking man. I am sorry this happened to you and I think we can figure out a plan."

She explained the tyranny of Workers' Compensation retraining in an educational way. Imagine, she began—a truck driver and a professional violinist both lose their right pointer finger at work. For the violinist, his whole life, his career, goes topsy-turvy. All that education, all that talent . . . wasted. What can he do? Not file a lawsuit. He petitions for retraining. He receives money for retraining because he has no prior work experience. He uses the money and his skills as a professional violinist to build a business as, say, a teacher. But the truck driver? He can drive pretty much the same so his work isn't severely impacted. After retraining (or for the truck driver, no retraining) is administered, the claim closes and both injured workers earn three thousand dollars in compensation for their Permanent Partial Disability, the cost associated with the loss of a finger. In that way, there is no discrimination for individuals. In that way, there is no special treatment for educational background or potential for earning power.

We learned that the Department of Labor doesn't have a specific category that serves to identify specific losses around living with a traumatic brain injury. I can imagine that it's pretty complicated to measure the brain without samples of what one looked like before the blunt force trauma. Still, it never seemed dignified to me to treat the back-to-work recovery of a patient diagnosed with a 'mild' TBI based on his or her educational or socioeconomic background. Vocational rehabilitation specialists must skirt around any cognition issues the traumatic brain injury *may or may not have caused* (how do we know he wasn't like this before?), angling instead on quantitative data as straightforward as pieces of missing limbs, bladder dysfunction, respiratory issues, nasal septum perforations, etc. I suppose it's easier to slice up the body's little visible parts than use a combination of time and research to analyze to what degree a person's specific residuals from a traumatic brain injury will affect their livelihood. How is it OK for a person who lost his toe be treated the same as a person who lost partial functionality of his one and only precious brain?

Bobbi suggested Matt look for an office job while we waited for the paperwork to go through. He was worried filing papers wouldn't be enough of a salary to support a family. She was honest, telling him, "Sadly, that's not the state's concern."

"What about this helicopter pilot's license you have?" she asked, looking through his three-inch-thick medical file.

Matt pointed to his permanently dilated pupil and said, "The FAA won't let me fly."

It was the eye, and it was also the seizure disorder.

"But I was thinking about computers," he said. "I'm good with computers."

Bobbi clapped with glee. Her homework would be to research reasonable and stable earning potential for entry-level web designers across the state, and then develop a proposal for three imaginary work situations. After that, she would send them to us for approval, then pass them through the familiar triangle of bureaucracy—Workers' Compensation, Harborview Medical Center and the University of Washington. Our small mouths opened for this morsel of generosity. We were little fish nibbling at food flakes beneath the surface of a pond.

Another specialist, the one holding the reins to our imagined freedom from the chains of insurance claims, was Dr. Feinstein, the young physiatrist in charge of Matt's rehab. She was around our age and I could tell she really liked Matt.

Every time he went in for a visit she treated him like a whole human. She looked over the same survey about drinking and smoking and depression he filled out every time, rather than have her interns do it. After four years, we were bored of the Workers' Compensation system and ready for Matt to tear back into real life. She was intrigued with what Bobbi had set up for retraining.

"I'm glad this is working out for you. A desk is where we want you to be," she said, serious-like.

I thought about how my dad had reminded me that the competition was tight for a career in web development in the Seattle area. "Why not stick to what Matt knows, like landscaping or carpentry? We will buy him a truck, a business license, equipment," he had said.

"*You* tell him that, Dad," I told him.

While we waited for Bobbi's plan to go through, Dr. Feinstein wanted Matt to test his stamina by volunteering fifteen or twenty hours a week. Did he have a friend with a business who could assign him light desk duties? It was a tall order for someone whose job had been healing at home. But we were lifted by the plan, encouraged to beat the odds.

Years later, when I published an essay about our journey in a national paper, I reached out to Dr. Feinstein, asking her to be my friend. She did write back, thanking me for highlighting the problems with how the public views traumatic brain injury, how recovery is much longer than a year. I still have the note. In it, she also told me she wouldn't meet me for coffee, that she couldn't cross those lines as a professional. Did she know something I didn't? That our journey was nowhere near over?

Though she never said so, I believe the doctor was saddened to see us back in her office a year after we had finally closed the L&I claim. Matt had struggled with employment and what I thought was clinical depression and PTSD. His headaches were excruciating. She knew more stuff about brain injuries and I knew more stuff about caregiving. She did not have the answers I desired.

We went to the Brain Injury Alliance of Washington's free community meeting and sat by a man who had been nearly killed by a drunk driver twelve or so years back. He was a doctor, or had been—I'm not sure which kind. At the free community meeting the former doctor wore a Hawaiian-print button-down shirt and khaki shorts and asked us about our accident story, though he was more interested in telling his own. Had he not been in Hawaii, had he been on the mainland, his medical treatment would have been superior and he wouldn't have been left in the street passed out in his own brain bleed for four hours too long. The doctor had lost his practice, his wife, his kids. Matt and I felt he was worse off than Matt, what with his stutter and word-finding issues, but to be fair, like Matt, he looked OK. He was active with the Alliance the way I wished Matt would rally around the cause. With his impressive-seeming recovery I felt he could inspire the community and make waves as an advocate. I pictured trips to Olympia to lobby legislators. I pictured public speeches and fundraising. It was more important to me than to him, though, so I dropped it.

The Alliance at this event had a free library where I picked up a memoir by Dr. Jill Bolte Taylor, a neuroanatomist who documented her own massive stroke in her lovely book,

My Stroke of Insight: A Brain Scientist's Personal Journey. I would discover later that her TED Talk was the first to go viral on the internet and when I watched it I cried. I promise, you will too. On minute thirteen or so, she becomes extra animated and emotional, explaining her awareness of her consciousness, saying it slowly, knowingly, that "just like a balloon, with the last bit of air, I felt my energy lift, and just, I just felt my spirit surrender. And, in that moment, I knew that I was no longer the choreographer of my life, and either the doctors rescue my body and give me a second chance at life, or, perhaps this was my moment of transition."

I sent a link to the TED Talk video to everyone who had survived our trauma with us, just as I did the documentary about 2010 Winter Olympics–bound pro snowboarder Kevin Pearce, *The Crash Reel*. Later a friend would have Taylor's book delivered to my home and I wouldn't have the guts to say I had already read it three times.

My nana, my dad's mom, was a big reader. She lost her husband to Alzheimer's, and she lost one of her daughters much too soon to cancer. She wrote poetry and once her children were grown she wrote two young-adult novels and an award-winning nonfiction book about early European settlers in the northwestern Detroit area. She had the best read-aloud voice I have ever heard. I was eleven when she gave me a draft of her manuscript to read. I was around the same age as her protagonist and I loved to read, so she wanted me to give her feedback and share notes.

I can't remember if it was Nana who insisted I read *All Quiet on the Western Front*, or if it was required reading in ninth grade, or if my dad wrapped it up one Christmas. *All*

Quiet was written by Erich Maria Remarque, a German veteran of World War I. Banned in Nazi Germany, it is a fictional story based on the author's personal experiences. It shows how fragile life is and how sobering war can be.

In it, a soldier home from war says, "I prefer to be alone, so that no one troubles me. They have worries, aims, desires, that I cannot comprehend. I often sit with one of them in the little beer garden and try to explain to him that this is really the only thing: just to sit quietly, like this."

This quote resonates with me when I think about Matt's experience, and in fact he expressed similar words when we fought.

"I'm just a woodsy guy," he'd say. "I am simple, and I don't need company."

I would push against this ridiculousness, arguing that he was a guy who chose *family*, and he was getting *better*. It hurt to hear his preference for being alone, and yet the idea of separating was starting to feel like a small relief. Not one I was ready for yet, but the seed was there.

"You need to accept the new me," he'd say.

He liked to smoke cigars and he'd smoke them as we stood on the back porch trying to figure it all out. I wasn't sure it was healthy for our family to accept his changes. It all felt so out of control, like banging your head against the same wall for the same reasons every goddamn day. Nonetheless, my sense of protection over him was stronger than my desire to pack the kids and go.

When you imagine the soldier's experience, the isolation returning from war, you can understand how solitude might feel better for someone who no longer feels connected to his community. Scornful sentiments enter the psyche; picture

Jean Valjean in Les Misérables returning from the chain gang. Neighbors, family, and old friends want to help, but you are changed. The inspirational redemption your community wants for you feels beyond reach. You are a cold and hungry wanderer peering through a window at a party from the outside. Matt didn't fight battles for our country, but the war analogy is the best way I can explain how a person might become so far away after a tragic accident affecting the brain and its emotions. It was lonely to know this and not be able to help. I bet my parents and friends felt the same about me: I had closed myself off to vulnerability, focusing mostly on the children's needs, often retreating into my own sober thoughts. Over the years I would recall the scene during rehab in the resident psychologist's office when Matt had described being lost in the desert with thirst for water he could see from afar, but could not attain. I knew there should have been comfort in knowing we weren't alone in these experiences, and yet I never found anyone to talk to who was the unhappy wife of a civilian with a brain injury tied up in a complicated Workers' Compensation claim. There was not a sense of forceful action in our issue, and the unique nature of the accident and its aftermath was exhausting to explain. I wished we could share in something like the collective national cry for a cure for cancer. Matt's fascinating medical case did not make me feel special.

Sometimes I turned to books about mindfulness to get calm. One I still like a lot is called *Peace is Every Step* by Thich Nhat Hanh. His philosophy is the same one expressed by the wonderful staff at the hospital. It is less offensive to me now, all these years later. Nhat Hahn tells me I can hold a light smile throughout the day, a little like the Mona Lisa, with the intention of banishing worry or fatigue. I try smiling lightly when I'm grocery shopping, or walking down the halls of the high school where I work. I don't worry if the other shoppers or teens think I'm foolish—I know at my age now how everyone is absorbed in their own lives. A hint of a smile relaxes my face and helps me return to the peace I have lost, the years I spent in anger and frustration. I do this for my benefit.

They said he should think like a *scientist*. They said he should practice *smiling* in the mirror. They ought to have encouraged the same for me. Had I been invisible? Where does a caregiver fit in? I try and do the smiling, just like I always mean to post sticky-note affirmations on my wall. I hear collecting rocks or feathers or shells is also good. Placing them on your windowsill helps you focus on a thing from nature first thing in the morning. This will have a grounding effect. A sense of calm means you are aware.

I can't locate my smile and I don't want to be grounded some days. That's OK too. As Thich Nhat Hanh comforts, your smile is there always, with a loved one waiting for you until you are ready to take it up once again. We can all take comfort in his words:

"Everything around you is keeping your smile for you. You don't need to feel isolated. You only have to open yourself up to the support that is all around you, and in you. Like the friend who saw that her smile was being kept by the dandelion, you can breathe in awareness, and your smile will return."

My peace wasn't always available to me that first year after Matt's accident, nor was it the years after when I felt it "should" be. It is good practice to offer the basic seeds for a practice in mindfulness—the breathing, the mantras, the smiling—but in my experience as a trauma survivor, the most valuable tool is knowing how to *hold* the in-between spaces. It is a confusing place to dwell. But, patience with ambiguity is the only way.

I learned to listen to myself say I would survive. I was lucky: the children provided me with a sense of purpose. For the gift of positive affirmations, I thank my parents, especially my mom, who instructed me on how to nurture myself with self-talk when I was young.

Patience with ambiguity doesn't come naturally to most. If you find yourself supporting a traumatized loved one, I would say this: refrain from offering confusing, unsolicited advice. The best thing a supporter can do is understand the strangling effect the culture's insistence on "getting over it" can have on mental health. It's OK to be sad, and grief is on-going. If I were able to talk to the self I was then, I would tell her to have faith. Faith in what you know to be your truth, even if it's unpopular.

Sitting with the unknown is about accepting that some-times there are no real answers, or no easy ones.

I was not born wise. I am what a therapist described in my early twenties as an "experiential learner." I do know that hurrying healing won't work. I also know that healing can happen, if you want it.

PART III

Once Matt's Workers' Compensation claim was closed, it was legal for him to earn money at a paying job. His vocational counselor recommended he apply for unemployment, an entitlement he could collect on while he attempted to find full-time employment. He received a structured payment for his Permanent Partial Impairment Award, some of which I negotiated with Joy when I read in the paperwork how Workers' Compensation would not acknowledge the specifics of his serious traumatic brain injury. I studied the Department of Labor Permanent Partial Disability Award schedules online and learned how these faceless monsters used something called TBI (Total Body Impairment) to determine figures for partial bodily losses as set by the consumer price index. Total Body Impairment hovers around $200,000, meaning in theory if you were completely disabled that's what you would receive, and yet this isn't true at all, because the way it works is if you are totally disabled you are entitled to a pension. Specific bodily loss is determined by the consulting physician in the independent medical exams, *the physician chosen by Workers' Compensation*, so for example, a Category 2 dorsolumbar and/or lumbosacral injury would be approximately 5% of TBI, which equals approximately $10,000. If the injury is determined to be a Category 8 though, that would raise it to 75% of TBI with an award of approximately $150,000.

You see where I am going with this. It's in the Department's best interest to secure low category ratings, if any at all. It's in the Department's best interest to select a physician who knows little about the injured worker's specific injuries. It is one hundred percent fact, for example, that the independent physician Matt saw for his anosmia did not want to believe Matt had lost his full ability to smell. Workers' Compensation is so massive that they *forgot* to schedule a psychiatric evaluation. If you do not steadily apply pressure to the doctors and claim managers, you are neglected. If you don't appeal, they will run you over. If you miss an appointment or are late, which Matt was once because of traffic and parking, it is perfectly within their rights to dismiss the exam and forgo that part of your award, the award you get for nearly dying.

This was a violent threat to live under. Sure, we called lawyers, but no one was interested in our case. For there to be a suit, Workers' Compensation had to have been negligent in paying time-loss, which they hadn't. Matt was robotic about his final payout, having battled an oppressive system for five years. He kept saying, "All I want is a fair shake." It made me consider our privilege as white people who have a command of the dominant culture's expectation for English. We had a mortgage and family who were educated and who could offer support. If Matt couldn't get what he considered a "fair shake," then what might be happening to people who didn't, by way of privilege, have access to navigate this terrible system that more and more felt like it was designed to hurt us? All the roofers who fall and break their backs on the job, all the housecleaners or seasonal fishermen and fruit pickers? How does the Department pick these consulting physicians? What are they paid to systematically ruin lives?

After Matt's series of independent medical examinations, we asked our community to digest with us this information: for his permanent lack of smell (anosmia), a seizure disorder, partial blindness, some "cognitive impairments," permanent facial numbness, and tooth damage, they awarded him in the end close to thirty thousand dollars. Nothing for pain and suffering, nothing for depression, nothing for loss of earning power and the expensive anti-seizure medication he would need forever. The award is meant to provide short-term care so that you can get back to paying taxes like a good American. The archaic Workers' Compensation system is designed to support industrial workers returning to *light duty* while they heal from a hurt elbow or broken finger—not for severe occupational injuries involving tree limbs crashing into skulls. And certainly, not for those poor workers severely and permanently damaged from inhaling toxic chemicals or operating heavy-duty machinery.

We had consulted attorneys about Matt's chance at earning a pension, which would secure a lifetime salary of his averaged earnings, same as the time-loss wages he'd received for nearly five years. It would be fair, we thought, since he'll never go back to helicopters or trees. But is he blind or maimed? Can he work, even if only a little? We consulted with professionals who said a pension was a long shot, so we forfeited the option and accepted the Permanent Partial Disability Award, plus several thousand dollars for school, which Matt made two separate attempts at but did not finish. After he got back to work and was unsuccessful, we began the process for his first application for

Social Security Disability Income (SSDI) for which he was denied twice.

Learning how those systems of brutality operate broke Matt and me down to a degree I could never have imagined. Maybe it's not my right, but I want to speak for both of us in saying it took years for either of us to feel part of the world again. We were so young to be faced with so much so fast. We dealt with a constant mound of paperwork without a certified social worker. Outside of doing right by the children, nothing felt right at all. It was as though with every Labor and Industries form letter that arrived we forfeited a degree of dignity. The same green Washington state stamp and cold government block typeface. It was impossible to forget how much we had lost, and were continuing to lose.

My parents were right to chafe at our spending some of Matt's Workers' Compensation Permanent Partial Disability Award on a vacation. I wrote a slick email, cc'ing my brother and his wife, saying, "Guess what! We got our money and we're going to Hawaii!" My brother was quiet on the other end, which was normal, but when my mother didn't respond, I thought, uh-oh. My dad called me twice from Detroit, where he'd been visiting his mother. He left a message.

"Your mother and I are disappointed in your choice to use that money for a vacation," he said. He wanted me to call him. We needed to talk.

It was a couple of different things: one, they would have never dreamed of indulging themselves like that, and two, we owed them money. It was reckless—I knew it. But it was our first vacation without kids and it sounded so sexy, like what everyone else who was normal always did. Outside of the accident itself, we had survived five years battling bureaucratic systems and we thought we deserved a break. It was also an attempt at saving our marriage.

Matt shrugged it off. He said, "It's blood money, and I want to have some fun." I argued (but only for a second) that maybe we ought to pay bills. He saw it as retribution.

Approval ratings for the trip were high among friends. In their eyes, we were *owed* a small slice of frivolity. I wanted to see it that way, too, like we were Sisyphus figures who had climbed the mountain with our boulders—our burdens—but unlike Sisyphus we were throwing our boulders from the mountain and having a party. I thought we must have earned the right to move on, and yet studying scripts in graduate school, I knew about false victories. A protagonist must think he's won in order for the last plot twist to have real meaning. I cringed every time a friend congratulated our achievements. I worried it was a jinx. My wiser parents understood our challenges ahead, and couldn't help lecturing us about how saving money is always smart.

Pinching pennies in Hawaii was a fun challenge. We got a hotel package that included a luau, breakfast, and two drink tickets plus a free towel for the pool. We ordered pizzas, made meat-and-cheese sandwiches and had chocolate-covered macadamia nuts and papayas for lunch. Matt had borrowed snorkeling gear from his dentist's receptionist, Barbara, who had grown to love Matt. (Workers' Compensation had paid the office she ran to have all his fillings replaced, his front tooth capped, and a bovine bone graft to replace a molar that had become infected beneath the surface.)

On the beach in my surfer-chick bikini, I looked like I belonged. Vacationers at their hotel saw a relaxed wife with moxie performing with luau dancers onstage. What they couldn't see was her pain at watching her husband depart for a day trip without a kiss goodbye. She looked like a tidy package, but how much longer could she possibly stay clean?

◆ ◆ ◆

UNDATED

Matt drove home wasted last night. He was late and I was texting him and he walked in the door all belligerent. It's really unlike him and I got super pissed. Before his accident, he never got this way when he drank. But he went to this holiday party or whatever for his friend's business where he volunteers and when he came home he was turning on lights and rummaging all around the house making all this noise and literally not making any sense when he talked. I pushed him away when he tried to get close and screamed at him about drunk driving. What if you had killed someone on the road—children or teens or a pregnant woman? He laughed in my face, slurring his words, saying that he wasn't even that drunk. He had been on the freeway, not just around the corner at the bar! He snored super loud and today of course he has to rest all day in the dark. I was so mad I couldn't sleep so I went to use the computer downstairs. I printed out graphic pictures of him after his surgeries at the hospital and also of our adorable kids' faces onto 8.5 x 11 paper and put them inside a little binder. I wrote a letter and gave both to him. It's not like an ultimatum but kind of. It's like he doesn't take anything seriously—it's all just a joke. Well, I don't think it's funny. We can't afford more tragedy.

◆ ◆ ◆

Matt ended up getting a part-time job at a trendy snowboard shop as a ski technician. He'd come home with bags of cool snowboarder swag, like stickers and sunglasses. He would complain that the kids at the shop didn't know what they were doing. "My boss is like, twenty-two," he'd say, all exasperated. The work dried up once the snow was gone and he was passed over for other jobs within the company he seemed qualified for. Later, he worked a construction job for a friend's business. He climbed tall ladders and inhaled toxic chemicals. He hauled off garbage and tore down drywall. I channeled my worrying into terrible prose and poetry. By midweek he would have "brain drain" and by Friday afternoon he was useless, lying in a dark corner somewhere with a terrific migraine. By summer the fatigue was so bad I called Joy Naveaga from Workers' Compensation to see about reopening the claim. "He is so depressed," I said. During a visit, Joanna saw it too. "Can't you get a lawyer?" she said, almost desperate. I just sighed, shook my head, and did the dishes.

Matt had never been your average middle-aged, pot-bellied Little League spectator. He was fit, with a clipboard, a Cardinals baseball cap, and a black windbreaker that said COACH KISHPAUGH in block letters on the back. He jotted drills in a notebook preparing the game's batting lineup. Sitting in the stands outside the field's fence I overheard a player's dad talking about Matt. He said to his wife how during practice this week Matt's fastball lesson in ball grip and accuracy was straightforward. He called Matt's coaching *remarkable*. It was not clear to me if he knew Matt was my husband. The man said, "The way Matt talks to the boys about the curveball is genius." He told his wife how Matt drew an airplane wing in the dirt, how he had traced an arrow over and under the wing to illustrate how a plane transfers speed into flight. He described how Matt had held the squirrelly boys' attention rapt as he connected the impact of high and low pressure on an airplane wing to that of topspin seam and speed. What a cool strategy, he said to his wife, to compare a curve in the air to the curve of a wing's top.

"It's really impressive how the science lesson made the boys pay attention," he said, and followed with a final fired-up exclamation that Matt was a really great coach.

Did the parents gather the degree to which a terrible accident had nearly cost this good coach his life? Were they more impressed by his coaching because they *did* know or had heard? Were they taken, were they awed, by his appearance of a full recovery? If they didn't know, all the better. I felt more and more conspicuous when people asked what Matt did for a living. I would stifle deep sighs and shift my butt around on the cold benches. I decided that when they asked, I'd say he knows all that stuff about velocity because he earned his helicopter's license when he was young. Then I'd change the subject and ask them about their job or daughter or dog.

◆ ◆ ◆

UNDATED

I drove to the hospital the other day. It was like my subconscious took over my body, steering the car toward James Street. I imagined a timber lorry semi in front of me letting loose a tree limb and crashing into the front dash. I whiffed the hand sanitizer. I swear, I could do the routine in my sleep—take the parking garage ticket, lock the car. I zombie-walked through the front revolving door toward the front desk lobby and past the east wing into the Malang building where I took the elevator to floor two, the ICU. I wanted to hug a charge nurse in blue scrubs. I just stayed in the shadows, imagining the families of the injured, how they were praying. I wandered around the floors locating the exact rooms where Matt's roommates Chit, Rod, Jake, Rick, Jon and Michael had lain and where I used to sit in the nubby orange chairs in the hallway while the kids were at the foosball table in the family room. I was in a half-awake state, thinking about where those guys are now, who might be loving them. Maybe somewhere in that hospital is a lost piece of me, so like a ghost I returned thinking I could claim it back.

✦ ✦ ✦

In breakup narratives, there are two, maybe more, sides to the story. It's hard to detail the sequence of events leading to our breakup; for me it may have begun with our first (and last) physical altercation.

I had purchased these business-size sticky notes from the office supply store and pasted them all over our house. Matt and I decided we would take a few hours to outline some goals—action items around financial stuff and career plans. I was already short with him after coming home from work to a torn-up backyard. We had discussed using a little money to reseed the grass, but I hadn't expected him to rent an excavator and begin the job on a weekday. I knew enough about these projects to understand how one thing would lead to another, and felt frustrated knowing he ought to be spending his time figuring out how to make money, not messing with machinery or further house improvements we couldn't afford. I pointed to the sliding glass door, accusing him of not wanting to face reality. I told him the yard looked like a war-torn minefield and he sniggered. I pointed at the posters and made a begging motion with my hands. Can't we please figure all this out? Can't we please make a plan? He narrowed his eyes and made a cold expression. I hardened my face. We engaged in a who-could-glare-harder contest until I let my anger take over and gave him a hard slap. His jaw pulsed and he reared up to give me a hard slap right back. I fell into the couch and held my burning face. I said, "I can't believe you did that," and began to cry.

He left and made arrangements to sleep at a motel that night. I poured a glass of cheap white wine into a plastic glass, walked outside and sat on the curb at the end of our cul-de-sac, where Lizzie was riding her bike. A neighbor approached me; she asked me if I was OK. I knew people shouldn't slap each other and that it probably wasn't something you were supposed to share. I just shrugged and pointed to our house. "I wish he were back to work," I said. She had once paid Matt to build a fence in her front yard. "I can understand that," she said softly.

I began to let go of thinking of our situation as something to solve. It was a slow untethering, bit by bit, from our union. It began when I could no longer sustain the hope of a full recovery, which cut into me a deep sense of shame. I had read all the books about traumatic brain injury, I had seen the documentaries. I fundraised for the local association and talked about Matt's miraculous recovery to anyone who would listen. But after five years, he couldn't manage consistent work, and that bothered me. It shamed me that it bothered me. It shamed me that I was so mad at him for not being himself.

In my writing program, I met new friends. I see this now as a necessary step in my own recovery. I needed to move beyond my frustrating suburban life and claim something just for me. Meeting people who didn't know what had happened was freeing, because I could be anyone I wanted. I could be a writer and party with my writer tribe.

I met a poet who turned me on. He took an interest in me and my writing. I didn't take an interest in him as much as I took an interest in the feeling of being admired. We exchanged messages about our projects. Then we texted. It was exhilarating to be talking about books and packet work and our dreams for how our manuscripts might shape up. It had been so long since I had engaged in intellectual discourse. I imagined myself writing a movie and I imagined a cover for this book, though I did not know yet how it would end.

Because the man lived far away, it felt innocent—not premeditated at all. There was an electricity between us, and when we saw each other in real life, we crossed the line, eventually having the affair we both wanted. If this were fiction

I would elaborate on the actual event and its aftermath, but it's not, so I won't. That's not fair to my family.

The affair was brief, but not meaningless, and I regretted going outside my marriage immediately. I knew I needed to move on, but I was scared how Matt would react if I claimed my life back. It's gross to think of myself as a cheater, but I would be a liar as well if I said the affair was the sole source of my shame. I knew I wanted to leave. The affair was an excuse. The shame came from years of excruciating loneliness. It came from knowing that I had had everything going for me—a husband, children, a house, an education—and wasn't happy. It came from the feeling that I had somehow not done enough to help him get better. If I had only studied law or business or medicine, then we might have enough money to throw at resources. We would have felt stronger, more connected with our contemporaries. It would take many years before I realized all I had learned, or gained, in losing.

I didn't tell Matt about my transgression. I simply stopped talking to him about anything much at all. I didn't neglect the children or my work, but I neglected him. It was like he had been this planet I had been orbiting, but now I wanted to be still, be my own orbit. We stopped connecting; we stopped having sex. I rolled my eyes when he spoke and changed the subject when friends and family asked how he was doing. A friend's husband had to urge me to contact his doctor when they witnessed him struggling to put together sentences one day after work. Any reluctance to help Matt was so unlike me; I had always gone to bat for him no matter what. When he quit the job working for a friend of mine's contracting business, we visited his therapist. She pulled me aside and asked point blank if I was done.

"It happens all the time," she said. "When women in weakened marriages go to graduate school, they meet someone else," she whispered.

I didn't give up any dirt—I wasn't sure what she would do with the information. It was in Marla's office where he announced his plan to go to Diamond Peak for a few months. She looked at me; I looked at her.

I shrugged. "At this point," I said, "I don't really care."

I'm not sure if he knew it was the end when he packed his bags, but I did. I did not try to convince him to do otherwise. We told the kids he would live at the Lodge until Christmas. He would work as a caretaker for his grandparents' property. In sitting the kids down, he wanted to tell them we didn't love each other anymore. I called my mom sobbing and she called Matt and helped him craft a softer version, which he read to them in a difficult moment of family truth. He would be better in Diamond Peak, he said. He needed some time to rest. Both children quietly wept. He left the day before school started and we didn't hear from him for six weeks. Unemployed now, after I got the kids up, fed, and off to school, I went back to bed. I spent the day staring at the ceiling, berating myself for having given up.

The man and I didn't get caught—not right away at least. His wife discovered the affair and contacted Matt. He confronted me and I admitted to the betrayal.

From there, his sadness turned to anger and he initiated the inevitable paperwork for a divorce. There weren't a lot of fights at this point—a few heated emails and mean texts—but mostly we were tired. Once I was caught, he insisted I bring the family to live in Diamond Peak, and though guilt tugged on me hard, I knew that this was the turning point in my life where I would be the one to support our family. It wouldn't be right to live in a cabin in the woods with no savings, no jobs, and a shitty relationship. I told no one about my affair but two old friends, calling one up on the phone slobbering on about how I was an adulteress, and she assured me it was going to be OK. She did not try and convince me to work any harder than I already had to keep this marriage alive. Another friend patted me and said, "I can't believe you waited as long as you did, to be honest." Matt shared my indiscretion amongst his close friends and family, and I can understand the need to do so. I was not beyond reproach in the breakup, and though I didn't go around sharing my ugly part, I steered friends away from thinking he was a jerkoff for leaving his family. The script might read one way, but it is always more complicated than it seems, perhaps especially so with a unique deal like brain trauma.

I explained it to my daughter, when she asked for the details years later, like this: I am not perfect. It was hard taking care of two kids, myself, the house, and a job without the support of a healthy partner. I borrowed the phrase my divorced friend suggested I use when she explained to her tween kids her split with their father: *My decision has had a negative effect on your life, and I'm sorry about that.* Both kids know about my cheating. They have heard me say that I couldn't reconcile the changes in our marriage, and how this has nothing to do with their relationship with their dad. They've been through so much that to be anything but honest would be to deny them the credit for surviving that they deserve. They both bring up the before and after. "I don't really remember anything," Isaac will say. And Lizzie will say, "I just know him how he is now." And that's exactly right. I sometimes wonder, was it never meant to be for us? I mean, we were so young. Would we have eventually separated, with or without the devastatingly stressful years of a "recovery"? There's no answer to that question, or if there were one, it's so dark that I prefer to hide behind the narrative that says that he changed; he didn't love me anymore.

◆ ◆ ◆

UNDATED

Matt came back from Diamond Peak saying stuff I don't believe he even means but I'm getting to the point where I don't care, like I can't fight anymore. He hates it here, everyone is a jerk. It's cheaper there, and he's a mountain guy and our house is falling apart and he doesn't like my path, this furious writing and reading I've chosen. The kids were upstairs singing "Rock the Kishpaugh" like I taught them, and he softened a little as we stood in the laundry room, saying he felt like a failure and he also just wants to be alone. I think what he means, and what it is too hard to say, is he needs a slower pace of life. But for your man to tell you he doesn't need human connection? Does that mean he prefers the woods to me—to us? Or have I inched so far away that this harsh talk is his way of protecting himself from what is looking like the inevitable? I keep thinking about what Molly's boyfriend said to me: be GLAD my life is so shitty because then life goes slow. I cannot WAIT for when life feels fast again!

◆ ◆ ◆

It was tricky finding work I could care about. I think it was because I was having a hard time coming down from all the adrenaline of living through some pretty high-stakes circumstances. Everything seemed so dull and insignificant. I turned down a job as an account manager for a firm that organized housing for foreigners working temporarily in the US, and I passed on a development associate role for the Brain Injury Association of Washington. I slept and cried, drove the kids to practice, drank wine. I wrote crappy little stories with no arc whose protagonists didn't want anything other than to be healthy again. It made me feel a little closer to Matt in the days when talking was not an option. This one never had a title. I guess I'll call it "Man in the Woods with a Headache."

Man in the Woods with a Headache

It was New Year's Eve and the children and neighbors were loud. Josh wasn't supposed to drive, but he started up the Explorer anyways, shutting out the noise from upstairs. He slid the SUV out of the garage, put it in four-wheel drive, and held his breath as the tire treads made that snow crunching sound he loved. A single inch of powdery fresh snow and he watched the tracks he made from the rearview window. He *knew* what Kate would say when she realized he'd ditched the party. *Leaving your own party, Josh? Really?* She'd shake her head in disgust when he didn't apologize. He admitted to himself that leaving a note might have been nice. His plan was to be right back; he only meant to get to the store for more beer.

He took the same back road he and his buddies grew up using. He cracked his one can of beer and put it between his legs. A lit cigar warmed his lungs and he took a hard drag, trying to remember what nicotine and evergreen boughs and snow even *smelled* like. The station on the radio was playing a classic rock countdown. He had missed last year's hits and was curious how the old, tired-sounding DJ figured this year's top ten songs. Picturing the man behind the speakers was easy: balding and scruffy in a trashed, post-holiday party office, lonely from all the imposed cheer. Josh wanted to pat that old guy on the back and say: *It's OK, man, it's nice the way you talk to us at night. Keep at it, man. These songs still matter.*

The neighborhood where Josh and Kate bought a house a decade ago was filled with '60s split-levels and this time of year they were all strung with Christmas lights. Out front were wide lawns and ample street parking. The Christmas lights that flashed hurt his eyes, and he felt a headache coming on. He wished he could be sure if the headaches came on just because, or if they were a result of his accident. Considering how Kate would likely overreact, asking her what she thought about it was out of the question. Those days she needed a lot of reassurance, which was irritating. He shrugged. *Oh, well.* He had plenty of concerns he didn't share with her. Like how on Christmas he couldn't figure out how to assemble Gus's Naboo Star Fighter Lego set. Or how the directions for an IKEA dresser drawer confused him. She hadn't noticed how he'd given up on both projects. The pieces were like a wall he couldn't hold up. If his life were a report card, he was earning a failing grade. Doctors told him he could get better if he tried. He could pass, if he did his homework. He sipped from the can. It was salty. One night off, that's all he wanted.

Everyone always wanted to know how Josh was *feeling*. He couldn't put words to it, except that since the hospital he felt like he was alone in the desert. Thoughts were loose sand he brushed from his leg. It made him angry and afraid. When he told the psychiatrist at the hospital he couldn't *feel* anything, Kate's eyes had bulged out like a fish caught on a line. *OK, so this is your homework*, the young psychiatrist had said. *I want you to practice smiling at yourself in the mirror, even if you don't think anything's funny.* Josh checked his face in the rearview mirror. He practiced grinning. It hurt.

At least he had his Atomics strapped overhead, the studded tires crunching underfoot. He was a night wanderer, a forest thief, snowflakes like jewels. Before they became men, his buddies would take this route, speeding over black ice. They used to love telling stories. Adrenaline pumped hot and it was impossible to tell whose tale was truer, or less a lie, than the next guy's. This was before families and jobs, decades before Josh's accident.

The highway was a single-lane death trap. Josh imagined telling that sad DJ how the railroad companies carved Highway 2 for carrying logs over the Cascades. How before that, the Tulalip tribes inhabited the land. How there was a time when the elk roamed free and silver, chum, and pink salmon swam up the Skykomish. He wondered if the DJ was a skier. *He sounds like the kind of guy I'd go to the mountain with.* Josh passed the town of Goldbar: Population 352. He noticed a flashing sign indicating a fatality had occurred last week. He shifted gears and the engine groaned, a perfect dispute for the peace beyond the grinding metal of the vehicle, an argument against the silent night air. He climbed, passing through the town of Index: Elevation 1400 ft.

Stevens Pass was steep, rocky terrain. Alex, Josh's favorite skier buddy, had hit his head doing a daffy off a small cornice at Stevens when they were seventeen. He'd acted like it was no big deal. *My neck hurts*, he told everyone at lunch. *I think I jacked it up.* On the way back home, he had passed out. They thought he was tired. Really he had had an aneurism, but the bleed happened slowly, and he died in his mom's car on the way to the hospital later that night. Alex was the type of nice guy that parents all liked. He was the one who hollered when he did a daredevil trick. He was polite to girls and had wanted to be a forest firefighter, even predicting his own death driving home once from the pass. *Hey guys*, he told them. *If anything ever happens to me, make sure you play Fugazi at my funeral.* A serious guy, someone you could really talk to. Now the rest of those guys were busy with their families and jobs. Josh had recently called a few who still lived in the neighborhood. Ben, the womanizer Kate disliked, could never come with him to the hill. *What are you doing, man?* Ben had asked. *You OK?* It was better to be alone, Josh thought, a beer between his knees, the soft murmuring of an old, tired nighttime radio DJ.

So much had happened in a year. His life was far away and he had trouble sorting things out. Kate was always halfway weeping, and Alex was long dead from that aneurism. He shrugged again. *What can you do?* Josh steered toward the next 500-foot elevation gain into Sultan, letting the heater blast his freezing feet. He had his Stanley canister, retrieved by Joe from the scene of the accident, and he was careful handling the wheel as he poured himself a cup of hot coffee. What he didn't have, and what he *really* wanted, was his double-layer, boiled-wool Filson vest. Emergency room physicians had cut it into rags, the bastards.

Josh mourned the loss of his favorite piece of work attire, but not as much as he missed his mole. He hadn't noticed until he'd been home for a week after rehab. He'd been concentrating in the mirror on how his one dilated pupil made his whole face look lopsided, when he noticed a scab behind his left ear. *What happened to my mole?* he'd asked Kate. She hummed over the sink and wiped her hands on her apron, ignoring him. *Kate. My mole. It's gone.* She examined the area behind his ear and rolled her eyes. It wasn't a big thing. *Maybe it got in the way of the stitches when they were sewing you up*, she said. *They were probably doing you a favor.* Kate shrunk into the kitchen and drew out her words when Josh asked how, exactly. *Well, big moles can be cancerous, so maybe removing it was preventative.* His little brother and his mom had been hovering unnecessarily in the living room. Josh didn't like the way the three of them peered at each other like they were in on a special secret. Josh growled and said, *Well, they didn't ask.* He looked at his brother, who was grinning at Kate, in on the joke. *Yeah, bro*, said Cory. *We should ask for that back.*

The Snoqualmie forest was protected national forest. Josh watched the forest quiver with the cutting wind as he slowed for the curving of a tight corner. A great horned owl rested in the crown of a silver fir, the liquid from its black round eyes boring into him as he passed it by. Two Cascade wolves loped inquiringly against the trunk. What he should do, he thought, is pull over and find that bottle of aspirin. His head was *killing* him. All those damn blinking lights. He pressed the accelerator and imagined the summit.

It was getting dark but he knew *exactly* in which direction he was traveling. A human compass, Alex used to call him. It seemed he hadn't lost the skills he picked up doctoring trees and flying helicopters. If Alex were here, he thought, they'd talk about the time Josh had saved them from getting lost when they'd spent the summer planting trees. Alex would have taught him about the mountain pine beetle epidemic. They'd nod and grunt and finally boast about their new skis. Maybe they'd even light up a jay. It would be easy talk, simple. He wouldn't have to describe what had happened the day he almost died, or about how he can't remember much of anything. Not like at home with Kate, his mother, and the kids, where it was loud, and everyone was curious.

The cell phone in the center console buzzed and his head throbbed. He passed a milepost that said, Stevens Pass: 10 miles. The classic rock DJ sounded old and tired. There were two songs until the top ten began and an hour until midnight. Josh plugged a set of electric boot warmers into the cigarette lighter so they'd be warm by the time he reached the hill. He cracked his window an inch and lit a Swisher Sweet. He checked the rearview mirror and glimpsed an imagined Kate, the joy in her face so real it reminded him of the picture he had of her taped against the inside of his tool box. *I hate that one*, she had said about it, and tried to peel it off. But the daydream only lasted a second. A shadowy object the size of his boot bag dropped in from the dark night and he made a little yelp even though he knew it was an owl. Josh tapped the brakes gently and manhandled the wheel like he always had in the dark night with snow, with the grace of someone tied to the land. He glanced at the rearview mirror but the creature was gone.

I stopped taking the depression pills because I thought they were making me fat. I wanted to keep trim after the separation; my jeans were loose for the first time in years. I emailed the nurse practitioner who had prescribed the Prozac for me, along with the Alprazolam, which I feared were habit-forming—that didn't bother me as much as the idea of them not working. I admitted to her that when the kids had gone to see their dad I stayed in bed for a whole week. I asked her if there were natural remedies she could recommend and she told me to look into something called Kavinace, available online. I looked it up and it was fifty bucks too expensive for me. She told me I'd had a rough time. She recognized I was "running on empty" and needed to fall apart for a little while, in addition to getting some sleep. She hoped some of these natural supplements would restore my energy and keep my skin as smooth as a baby's butt. She sent me links to other non-habit-forming supplements, stuff like phosphorylated B-complex, zinc picolinate, Epsom salts, Vitamins D-3 and B-9, using L-tyrosine or Focus D & L as needed for energy which would boost the Prozac. Had I asked my mom or a friend, they would have gladly bought all of these and more for me, but I was ashamed I couldn't pay for them, and I was ashamed of being so sad. Remember, she told me, these are time-limited events and that I must preserve my good looks at all costs. Depression ages a woman faster than a tanning booth, she said. She signed off with the Five Commandments for Taking Antidepressants.

Dear Sarah,

Rule No. 1: Never stop taking an antidepressant in winter in the Northwest. Wait until summer.

Rule No. 2: Never stop taking your antidepressant if you are going through a divorce, even if it's summer.

Rule No. 3: Never stop taking your antidepressant—even in summer—if you are getting a divorce while going to graduate school, until a sane person tells you to stop.

Rule No. 4: Never stop taking your antidepressant if you are getting a divorce, going to grad school AND raising children alone, even if it's summer and even if a sane person tells you to stop.

Rule No. 5: Never stop taking your antidepressant if you are getting a divorce, going to grad school, and raising children alone—even if it's summer and a sane person tells you to stop. In fact, under these circumstances, ADD a tranquilizer like Xanax as a rescue medication as needed.

✦ ✦ ✦

(a letter)

Hey.

Hey, remember the lilac bush our older neighbor Andy gave us the first spring after we moved into the second house? When the sun came out she was out there with a hand mower every day. You nicknamed her the "mow-ho," but you admired her gardening skills. We kept the barren plant in an orange tub from Home Depot for like two years. It bloomed every year in April, these white blossoms that smelled like hope. You planted it along the side of the fence, in between the different variet-ies of plum trees. Since you've been gone it's gotten bigger. The apple tree needs pruning. The fruit is small and the shoots are wild. I know I'm supposed to do it in winter, but since you left, I rarely go in the backyard when it's wet or dusky. The pear tree blew over in a storm last fall. Its root base lay looking up at me, exposed and raw, as if to say, this wouldn't have happened had *he* been taking care of me. I left the leafy remains there until spring, when I hired a guy to come chop it up and take the debris to the dump. I had forgotten how large stumps look on the ground versus when they are upright and living. I was cutting down the cedar branches by the fence today. I wanted to let in more light in the yard and it seemed doable. The vine maple you planted in the root stump is doing OK; not thriving, exactly, but alive.

The little fir tree Isaac gave you as a seedling for Father's Day is bigger now, nearly three feet high. Remember, he gave it to you in burlap sack that fit in your palm? You planted it in the front yard in full sun. The crocosmia, bee balm, barberry, rhubarb—they are flourishing, I think because of the gold dirt you brought in from the good nursery. The rosemary and mint and thyme you stuffed between the granite rocks you laid are looking good. I ought to use them more for cooking—ha ha, now I know you're laughing! The tenant downstairs dug up the periwinkle hydrangea to fill up a barren area out front. The extra space adjusted itself so the small Japanese maple can now soak up sunlight usually hidden by those Western red cedars that give us privacy alongside the back fence.

Every time I'm out there I channel you. There are piles as I write, piles of debris from a summer windstorm I will gather and cut and stuff into those tall paper sacks from Lowe's and put on the corner when it's yard waste day. I am gaining momentum, since it's been a while now. At first I couldn't bear to use a single garden tool, but now I am a machete artist. After you left I ended up selling the big ornamental ceramic pots for some cash, but when the lady from Craigslist asked if the baby blue one was for sale, I said no way. I keep the hose in it still. That was a nice gift you gave me; I love how smooth it is, and the color reminds me of a robin's egg. So was the wisteria, which is flowering now (finally). It's nestled in between the bamboo you planted (also taking over) and the lavender. I want to dig it up and put it out front so I can enjoy it every time I walk down the porch and get in the car, but I can't bring myself to risk watching it wither and die.

◆ ◆ ◆

(a letter)

Hey.

Hey, remember the piles of money we spent at Dr. Lee's office? I went there today to get my teeth cleaned—first time in three years—and thought of you. Barbara was there and I told her before she could ask that you lived far away now. I made appointments for the kids and her eyes got big when I said Lizzie is thirteen and a half now. Remember the travel picture wall in the waiting room? We thought it was funny that Dr. Lee asked her clients to take pictures of themselves flossing on mountain tops or against a backdrop of Mayan ruins. Barbara showed me the picture of the four of us flossing with Donald Duck. It made me think of that trip, how we had saved and bought a package hotel/pass deal, how we lugged our store-bought food everywhere and that scary van ride to the airport, that lady van driver who drove like ninety miles per hour on the interstate even though one wheel was clearly busted.

At Dr. Lee's there was a glossy hip magazine with a title on the cover that said, "Best Winter Spots in Seattle." Guess what it was a picture of? It was a group of handsome, earthy-looking thirty-somethings sitting around an outdoor fire pit I recognized as the spot adjacent to the restaurant where we hosted our wedding reception. After the teeth cleaning, I was relieved Dr. Lee didn't have time to do my exam. She would have likely asked about you, unlike Barbara who is perhaps extra sensitive to client needs and also had a pretty good relationship with you. Barbara did say in reverence how you and I had gone through so much together. After Dr. Lee's, I went to the store and bought a small bottle of Crown and remembered how we would drink our holiday drink, a little Crown with Bailey's.

Another thing: everywhere today—walking up to Barbara's reception desk, strolling down the aisles at the market, or chatting with colleagues at school—I got compliments on my rain jacket. Oh, this is more than a rain jacket, I told them—it's a *ski* jacket. It's the one you bought me, remember, solid black except for the thin pink stripe along the arms? It's been dumping rain this winter but it keeps me warm and stylish. The dentist, the magazine, the jacket, the drink—it's odd how the connections are becoming distant. These days I think about the *why* less than before and I know I'll never send these letters to you but I need to write them for me, just to say that it wasn't all bad, despite what we had to survive.

◆ ◆ ◆

I feel like it's OK to say I was married to the same man twice. There was no ceremony to commemorate the second marriage, no funeral to mourn the first one's loss. I offered once that Matt and I should spiritualize our loss every year on October 30 by burning something important, like medical charts or letters from the state, then sprinkling the ash over the pier at our beach. I can't remember what he said but if I were to guess I'd say he made a joke about making sure to bring the crab pot and buoy.

I remember how after our Hawaii trip, back home in the cul-de-sac, Matt and I had accepted an invitation to a neighborhood dinner party processional. All the kids would stay in someone's basement playing video games and eating pizza. The processional was a Mexican theme and my part was dessert, so I made a *tres leches* cake. Matt and I were tan and relaxed. Matt told the story of how he'd bumped heads with Henry, the sea turtle that traversed Black Rock on Maui's Kaanapali coast.

"I can't see peripherally out of my right eye," he reminded everyone, pointing to his blinded area that made it so he bumped into pregnant women or the elderly, something that caused him great embarrassment. I remember it was *enchiladas verdes* for the main course and I can't remember what else. I remember it being a cheerful occasion, one in which I felt grateful to have a handful of tight-knit neighbors I could tell stories and share a book club with—one in which our children played with the others and we could laugh and drink and eat together during the holidays.

Two years later would be my first Christmas without Matt. The neighbors were kind to invite me to another processional, this time a French theme. I made it to the wine and cheese part and had to go home. It was depressing, the men in holiday sweaters and the women all gussied up. The houses smelled like too-strong candles and I wasn't eating anyway, so what was the point? They understood and no one gave me grief. I walked home and binged on wine and movies and cookies. Then I wrote a short piece called "How to Break Up with a Brain-Injured Man." It was therapeutic.

How to Break Up with a Brain-Injured Man

Take a chapter from your yoga girlfriends' book and Simply Be. Pretend you're a scientist and observe his rehab with interest. When the stress makes you scratch at your scalp until it bleeds, see a nurse practitioner. Don't be shy about asking for a prescription for Xanax. You'll say: But I don't like taking pills! She'll say: Now is when they're *meant* for.

No one appreciates a quitter. Lobby for his Workers' Compensation entitlements. Getting hurt on the job means he will receive one hundred percent medical coverage. A mild brain injury is tricky—the mind is cloudy but on the outside one looks only slightly off. Urge him to attend a group meeting for brain injury survivors. Ask the hospital to fax over the entire ten pounds of medical files and submit a request for an accident report. Make copies for yourself and keep them organized in a small file cabinet in the basement by your desk. You never know when you might need them for a story.

Tell Heather, the manager of membership and marketing of a significant-sounding resource, that no, you won't be attending next year's conference. Respond one last time that you are not interested in the webinar on Managing TBI-Related Stress and Anger. Turn off your Google alerts for Traumatic Brain Injury and unsubscribe to the Patient Advocate Institute's weekly e-newsletter. When they pester you for donations, you'll want to say: I'm moving on. Try to refrain. It will inspire neither admiration nor sympathy, so what's the point?

Getting caught with a lover would make you the bad guy, which sounds like an easy out, but don't do that. It doesn't matter if you spent one year or ten nursing your man back to life—he's a guy's guy and men like him get badges and awards. Which is why you have to be honest. Say: It's time to cut our losses. Don't be shocked when he agrees. Put your arm through his and stroke his bicep. Let him snap nude pictures of you and give him one last blowjob. Swallow so he knows you still love him.

When he does leave, do the following:

Go first thing in the morning to the local Department of Social Services and apply for food stamps. It will take all day, so bring a book and charge your phone. Be gracious to whoever walks you through your new client interview. Say: You are so nice. This must be a hard job. Smile with all your teeth. Don't be ashamed when they ask if you need Temporary Assistance for Needy Families. This is Welfare. Take it. Refrain from sharing this news with your man. His pride is still so huge and you don't want to deal with a suicide.

Tell a dear friend you need her to hold your hand at the food bank. Try not to turn your nose up at the massive bags of lentil beans and molding vegetables. There will be frozen whole chickens and white bread, blocks of cheddar cheese, and four-day-old pastries. Don't forget the sundries station—it is surprising how fast shampoo, toothpaste, dish soap and toilet paper run out.

Give his claims manager a heads-up he's leaving. Email his medical team, starting with the rehabilitation director. It's not likely she'll respond, and if she does, don't expect a warm exchange. Contact his eye doctor, speech therapist, psychologist and neurologist. They will want to know the details but they won't ask. Tell yourself managing their disappointment is not your job.

Call a renowned psychotherapist and get on her waiting list. With your last one hundred dollars, purchase a holistic body-work session or two—they should get you feeling like a woman again. Phone the kind ladies at St. Vincent de Paul for help with the utility bills and groceries. Schedule the visit for when the kids are in school. Declutter the living room and stash the Modern Warfare games behind the TV. Tell them your story, let them pray for you, and cry on their shoulder.

Take yourself to as many parties as possible. A prudish acquaintance might ask twenty questions at a gift exchange party. She will suggest you wait until you're legally divorced to date or sleep around with anyone. Be grateful when your twice-divorced friend interrupts and asks the woman if she has been through divorce. Oh no? Well. Both of you need to leave it at that. Take your ally by the hand, thank her and ask her if she wants to smoke a joint. Puff in a corner of the backyard by yourself if she says no thanks. Who cares?

Inform your man's best buddies on the haps vis-à-vis private messages on Facebook. Consider blocking your man's access to your posts. Does he really need to see all the pretend fun you're having without him? Tell yourself: You are good, You are good, You are good. Try a self-hug—those are nice. Warm a hot-water bottle to snuggle with in bed and take a bath every single night. Light a candle and ask yourself: Self? What do I want?

If mystery is your style, compose a macabre email to your friends outlining how you are falling to pieces. BCC handfuls: the ones who have forgotten you and the ones who won't leave you alone. Tell them that in case they don't hear or see from you in a while, it's because you are benching yourself. Say to them: I need three months. Say to yourself: After that, I will be better.

Relinquish the roles over which you have grown accustomed to wielding control, for example, the ongoing claim for his workers' compensation damage award or his application for Social Security disability benefits. Crafting an informative email identifying everything you know about the bureaucracies with which you've dealt over the years will secure your position for primary custody, but you needn't worry about that. You both know no judge will give him the kids.

For your first Christmas without your man, pre-forgive yourself for overdrinking. This is *your* year, the one for which people, even your mother, ought to forgive any belligerence. If having a friends' holiday is an option, do that, and bring nothing except yourself and a bottle of something you plan to finish. Likewise at your neighborhood dinner party processional, if looking at the couples in Christmas sweaters spreading cheer makes you want to hide in the bathroom puking over a cinnamon-scented Yankee candle, politely tell the host that you are not up to it this year.

If possible, on Christmas morning, instead of church, attend one of those Lonely Hearts Club prayer sessions. Don't think of it as a-misery-loves-company-type deal, but a natural part of the grieving process you endure with like-minded humans whose hearts feel like they may collapse at the sound of another carol. Let the grief soften your structure. Say: Tomorrow is a new day. Breathe.

Walk to a neighbor's house, those musical geniuses who don't have children, for a very dirty martini stirred especially for you. Listen to jazz on vinyl and read their Dennis Leary's *Merry Fuckin' Christmas* coffee-table book. If, when you crawl back to your house bleary-eyed, your children have put themselves to bed, chocolate smeared across their faces and their Christmas dinner clothes still on, don't feel too bad. You've made it this far. Keep going.

As for dating, don't jump into anything too soon. Play the field, have phone sex, make out at the bar, but dear God, *do not* cohabitate with anyone for at least two years. That old flame? When you feel like calling him, simply make tea, take half your Xanax and read surrealist literature until you pass out. It may feel like you want to worry and clean and cook for someone, but a warm body will not stop your witching-hour adrenaline rushes, so what would be the point of putting your kids through having a strange man in the house? Just wait. Your happy ending is on its way.

When you're packing your man's stuff be sentimental to a point. Ask your most nonjudgmental friend over and together fold his messy clothes and put them into boxes. Keep the chocolate-brown suede Filson gentleman's jacket you gave him the fall he turned thirty. In a year maybe he'll remember. Give it back when he asks. For now, tuck it in the corner of your closet. Smell it from time to time when you need a reminder of his hunkish, sap-smelling neck.

Be fair and throw nothing out. Buy a box of large Ziploc baggies to store his miscellaneous personals: an old wallet with business cards and a 3x5 of your wedding photo; his expired helicopter license, some childhood marbles, an inscribed Swiss army knife, and his dad's U.S. Army pin; his wedding ring, a set of bonsai clippers, a set of 2.0 pencil lead and his favorite Staedtler mechanical pencil and sharpener, a Factis extra soft eraser, and the twisted brass bracelet you bought in Puerto Vallarta on your honeymoon; a handheld voice recorder machine, a Li-ion 3.7V battery for his ski helmet camera, and a book of matches whose logo of a pole dancer is underneath the tagline, *Steak and Legs*; a Hohner international harmonica in the key of C, a piece of what looks like a computer chip, inside a pink plastic baggie labeled "The Memory Place," and his arrowhead, styled into a necklace, that he found in the desert when he was ten.

The emergency epilepsy I.D. bracelet, the one with the weird American Medical insignia that's like a thick red star with a snake hugging a staff, is yours to keep. On the back are your name and number. He never wore it and won't miss it. Store it in the bottom drawer, along with the government memo identifying the date, time and details of injury. He may or may not keep the green silk satchel filled with good-luck charms stuffed last year into his Xmas stocking: a gourd, a four-leaf clover, a shooting star, a horseshoe, and a pair of dice. Just put them in the box. They are his.

When a foreign bitterness scorches your throat each time someone asks you to explain your tragic splitting-up story, remind yourself (silently) how you would not want to trade places with your man. His having left, his having gone away, his having *made room* for both of you to one day begin again, makes him a hero. Tell this to yourself over and over and over. Disregard friends and family who disparage his seemingly hasty departure. You know things. These are the things you know: *He* lost his smell, not you. *He* lost his eyesight, not you. *He* lost his memories, not you.

Chin up, you're halfway there.

BIOGRAPHICAL NOTE

Sarah Cannon grew up in the north-end suburbs of Seattle, and graduated from the University of Oregon with a degree in Spanish. She earned her MFA in 2014 from Goddard College where she helped launch the inaugural Lighthouse Writers' Conference and Retreat in Port Townsend, WA. Her work has been featured in the *New York Times*, Salon.com, *Bitch* magazine, and more. Sarah lives in Edmonds, WA with her family, where she is a freelance technical editor.